Kentucky Quilts and Their Makers

MARY WASHINGTON CLARKE

Photographs by Ira Kohn

THE UNIVERSITY PRESS OF KENTUCKY

Research for The Kentucky Bicentennial Bookshelf
is assisted by a grant from the
National Endowment for the Humanities.
Views expressed in the Bookshelf do not
necessarily represent those of the Endowment.

ISBN: 0-8131-0228-6

Library of Congress Catalog Card Number: 76-4435

A statewide cooperative scholarly publishing agency
serving Berea College, Centre College of Kentucky,
Eastern Kentucky University, The Filson Club,
Georgetown College, Kentucky Historical Society,
Kentucky State University, Morehead State University,
Murray State University, Northern Kentucky University,
Transylvania University, University of Kentucky,
University of Louisville, and Western Kentucky University.

Editorial and Sales Offices: Lexington, Kentucky 40506

Contents

Color Plates follow page 40

Preface

W_HEN I FIRST MOVED_ into a rural Kentucky neighborhood I was delighted to find that a near neighbor had been quilting for more than seventy of her eighty-four years. She has created more beautiful quilts than she can enumerate handily, and she is still quilting at the time of this writing. Over the years of our acquaintance I have watched her busy fingers hour after hour, my interest sparked by a lively quilting tradition in my own family.

Assisting in the preparation of a television documentary on Kentucky's quilting heritage in 1970, I actively solicited information from my neighbor, her neighbors, and theirs—my visits with notebook and camera spreading out over several counties of central and western Kentucky. And since I find it difficult to resist an attractive quilt if it is for sale, I accumulated a few unusual examples to grace the beds in my own home.

Following this interest has led me to many excellent books on American quilting. Some of these are splendid studies, capturing the riot of color and design in this active and expressive craft. I am impressed by the richness and variety of quilting in the country at large, and I am even more impressed by the fact that I can find in my microcosm of central and western Kentucky counties so nearly the full range of names, styles, patterns, techniques, beliefs, and customs associated with quilting. My travels outside this small area reinforce my conviction that the tradition is alive and well, flourishing in both urban and rural settings, with no apparent diminution as a younger generation accepts it and keeps it alive.

For my emphasis on a network of neighborhoods and

personalities I will give most of my attention to this microcosm that I know well and believe to be representative. The great advantage in a restricted view is that it makes possible a focus on some of the quilters as well as their works. Like a fingerprint, any quilt differs from all others in one or more ways. The object does not exist in a vacuum. If we could reveal all its mysteries, a quilt could tell us something of the memories, aspirations, small triumphs and defeats of its maker. It tells us much about her aesthetic sensibility, her skill, care, and imagination.

Rather than an extensive catalog of designs, therefore, what follows here is a sampling of Kentucky quilters, their work, and how they go about it. Unless otherwise indicated, the quilt names are theirs, the informal technical language of the craft is theirs (though the author must confess to some regularizing to avoid confusion), and the tools and approaches described here are the ones they prefer.

I wish to express my gratitude to Western Kentucky University for assisting with the publication of this book. Special thanks are due Riley Handy and the staff of the Kentucky Library; Patricia MacLeish, social science librarian, who facilitated my use of the Western Kentucky University Folklore and Folklife Collection; and Bruce MacLeish, curator of museum collections.

Others who gave valuable assistance were Miriam Gittleman Tuska of Lexington, Novella Wininger of Glasgow, and, of course, the quilt-makers listed in the index. The Kentucky Historical Society Museum provided the photographs of the Kentucky Graveyard quilt; and the Smithsonian Institution, the photographs of the Russellville Fair Grounds quilt. The informal photographs are from Kenneth and Mary Clarke's Kentucky Heritage collection. All other photography was done for this book by Ira Kohn.

1

"IT GIVES ME PLEASURE"

THE INVOCATION at a state-wide gathering of extension home economists in Lexington in 1975 was a passage from Eliza Calvert Hall's early twentieth-century novel *Aunt Jane of Kentucky.* In this passage a quilter used her craft as an analogy for living one's life, and the speaker adapted it effectively to fit her profession. Later, in the informal luncheon conversation, youthful home economist Donna Manning of Bell County remarked, "Quilting is really *in* now over around Cumberland Gap," affirming for her region that a craft significant in eastern Kentucky from its pioneer beginnings still survived and thrived there. "Do you know, I have discovered three quilters in the block where I live?" chimed in a resident of a Lexington neighborhood near the University of Kentucky campus. Novella Wininger of Glasgow, Barren County Extension agent for home economics and director of cultural arts in several counties of south-central Kentucky, announced that the quilting workshops she had been conducting in the area always attracted an interesting range of quilters. She predicted a bright future for this cultural art which has given so many women pleasure and a sense of accomplishment since the "great-grandma days." Reports of quilters and exhibitions of quilts from other parts of the state further demonstrated that enthusiasm for quilting was running high in Kentucky on the eve of the nation's Bicentennial.

Between 1970 and 1975, more than a thousand Kentucky quilters representing some twenty counties were interviewed and their quilts photographed or described for the Western Kentucky University Folklore and Folklife Collection. At festivals, fairs, and other craft exhibits across the state during that period, colorful and original quilts kept appearing in ever-increasing numbers. The nationwide crafts revival in all its diversity inevitably involved handmade quilts and their makers, as did the similar surge of interest in the 1930s. But quilt-making in Kentucky at least has never died—it has never substantially slowed down! At all times it has been responsive to influences from popular culture with the result that viewing the products both historically and geographically reveals almost infinite and continuing variety.

Some women prefer to quilt in church or community groups, some in families, and some alone. Their ages, resources, and rewards vary greatly—from the urban-based "Cornpickers" organized in the 1970s to make and sell quilts, to the lone quilter of sixty years' experience who has never sold one. But one thing they hold in common: they continue to quilt because "It gives me pleasure."

The Quilting Bee

The morning of April 19, 1975, was clear and sunny in Bowling Green, Kentucky. The old-fashioned two-story brick house at 1235 Chestnut Street was spotless in readiness for Thala Layne Thompson's birthday party. In one of the big old double parlors at the front of the house stood a large homemade quilting frame worn satin-smooth with long use and resting on sawhorses. Mrs. Thompson had "put in" a quilt. Tightly stretched in the frame with loose basting threads radiating diagonally from center to corners to hold the cloth "sandwich" firmly together was

2

a Double Wedding Ring, one of her favorite patterns. The rainbow of colors in the tiny pieces that formed the large overlapping circles was set against a background of lavender.

By nine o'clock eighteen women, all members of the Good Neighbor Quilting Club, had arrived. Each bore a favorite covered dish for the feast that traditionally follows the quilting bee—enough to load two tables with food, one for desserts alone. Other friends and members of the hostess's family, including several of the men, usually joined the quilters to enjoy the "eats." Brade Thompson, retired from farming because of a "bad heart," joined his wife in greeting her guests, then disappeared until noon.

Since 1936 Mrs. Thompson and her neighbors from the nearby rural Sharer Community, where she had lived until recently, had been honoring one another's birthday anniversaries in this manner. The hostess would piece the quilt and provide all necessary materials for completing it, happy to add another handmade quilt to her store as a birthday event. Mr. Thompson joked with the guests, "If she goes before I do, I want her to leave me plenty of quilts to keep me warm." And she retorted, "I don't plan to leave you a single quilt for your next wife to come in and use. Let her make her own!"

Three women seated themselves on either side of the quilt, the two rails of the frame spaced apart for a "reach" from both directions, a reach being the distance a quilter can easily sew from her seated position. As each reach is completed, the quilt must be rolled over one side of the frame to expose another reach until stitching has covered the entire quilt; it is then ready to "take out." To facilitate the rolling and to hold the quilt firm at all times, two holes had been bored into the supporting sawhorses, with corresponding holes through the frames so that a large "spike nail" could easily be inserted and withdrawn as necessary. "The quilt must be firm," Mrs. Thompson emphasized.

3

Figure 1. Members of the Good Neighbor Quilting Club at Thala Thompson's frame. Two reaches are exposed of Double Wedding Ring pattern against a background of lavender. 1975.

Some of the women had brought their thimbles and scissors and even their favorite no. 7 short quilting needles that would make tiny darting stitches through the three layers—top, cotton batting, and lining. These expert seamstresses like to feel along the underneath part of the quilt where the needle is going and keep the lining as wrinkle-free as the top. The forefinger of a quilter's left hand is almost an index to her skill, pocked or even slightly calloused. "Adhesive tape helps," Mrs. Thompson suggested, "but some of our members don't like to use it because they want to be sure they can feel the point of the needle getting through all the layers." Without seeming to hurry, the quilters gave credence to Warren County quilter Rose Brite's description of old-time bees: "We sewed with a red-hot needle and a burning thread!"

The Wedding Ring pattern lent itself to quilting variations, since the solid-color areas were fairly large. Mrs. Thompson sometimes "crossed" the background areas with bias lines or checks; at other times she quilted in them rather elaborate flowerlike motifs. Quilting "by the piece," as these women were doing, is popular throughout the state, and even when the pieces are very small it is traditional to "hit every piece" with the quilting design. The border, like the main part of the quilt, may be quilted to follow the pattern of the piecing or applique, or it may be quilted in rope, chain, vine, or floral motifs.

Mrs. Thompson had patterns, lead pencils, and a ruler at hand for laying out, or marking, the quilting design as they went along. Light pencil markings, she assured a newcomer to the club, would brush away after the quilting was finished. For some quilting patterns she made use of convenient household objects—a thimble for very small circles, a water tumbler for larger ones. "The width of a ruler is a good distance apart for bias lines," she remarked.

As the needles flew, so did the talk—news and gossip of themselves and their friends and families since their last gathering, perhaps as long ago as a month earlier. One of the women reminisced, "I can remember when we used to sleep under so many quilts you could hardly turn over!" She had grown up with her grandmother in a log house, since fallen into ruins, and remembered that in her upstairs room the snow sometimes sifted through the cracks on cold winter nights. "And now I use that electric blanket my kids gave me in a house all heated with a good furnace instead of a woodstove." But she still liked and used her quilts over the electric blanket, though not so many or such heavy ones. "I just wouldn't feel right without some quilts on my beds." Many of her fellow quilters have shared her experience of using modern conveniences for comfort while keeping the traditional bedcovers as a matter of taste.

The Good Neighbors, like traditional quilters throughout the state, were familiar with old beliefs and customs relating to quilts, but few of them expressed the beliefs or continued to observe the customs. Several of these beliefs relate to marriage. A girl should have a baker's dozen (thirteen), or some say twenty, tops accumulated for family and friends to help her quilt during the period between the announcement of her engagement and her wedding. Her special Bride's Quilt should be quilted entirely by others. She should do no more than shake it out after it leaves the frame. If a girl shakes a new quilt out the front door, the first man who enters will be her husband. The girl who puts in the last stitch of the quilting will be an old maid. The Good Neighbors did not know the warning given by several other Kentucky quilters—that if a single girl makes a Lone Star quilt she will be an old maid, or that it is just plain bad luck for anyone to make a Lone Star.

The most widespread custom, which several women present had actually practiced when they were young, was shaking the cat. When a finished quilt was taken from the frame the girls would put a cat in the middle of it. Four girls would hold the corners of the quilt and shake it. The one nearest to the place where the cat jumped out was expected to be the next to marry.

These and other beliefs appear to be widely known but lightly taken today. Never begin a quilt on Friday or you won't live to finish it. Don't quilt on Sunday or you'll have to pick out the stitches with your nose. Sleep under a new quilt and the dream you dream will come true or you'll have good luck. "Brade and I will sleep under this one tonight," Mrs. Thompson remarked with a smile, "so maybe we'll have some good luck."

The Double Wedding Ring could be finished in a day by good quilters, relieving one another at the frame from time to time. But Mrs. Thompson recalled her birthday of 1972, when it took three parties for the group to finish the more elaborately quilted Star of the Bluegrass. Most of the members considered work done by hand, or "on their fingers," superior to anything the machine could produce, whether piecing, quilting, or binding. For the finishing touch on this quilt Mrs. Thompson, wishing to accent the lavender of the top, had used a separate tape binding instead of turning the lining over onto the top. She stitched the binding to the underside, turned it so that the seam was on the wrong side, and finally stitched it to the top with nearly invisible stitches, following the large scalloped edges of the pattern.

Some members recalled the depression years of the 1930s, when quilt-making from scraps left over from clothing and household uses was simply a way of keeping their families warm. "It was plain old hard work and do-it-yourself," Mrs. Thompson said, speaking for all. They came from families that for generations had included good quilters. As the Good Neighbor Club completed its third decade in the nation's Bicentennial year, members looked back over the changes the years had brought—the deaths, the new members, the alterations in their way of life that had made their activity more social than functional. Why did they continue this painstaking activity past the time of necessity? Another quilter, not a member of the Good Neighbor Club, spoke for quilters throughout the land: "I quilt for a contented heart." A mood of contentment pervaded the Thompson household on that spring morning, not only at the frame but also where some who no longer quilted were busy piecing blocks and others were simply "stitching and chattering." (At Sebree in Webster County a quilting group named itself the Stitch and Chatter Club.)

Although the Good Neighbors' preference was for pieced work quilted in fans, checks, diagonals, and diamonds, Mrs. Howard (Mary) Thompson had involved the group in some elaborate quilting in feathers, flowers, and leaf designs on her own favorite appliqued patterns. Especially during their early existence as a club, their choices were governed largely by everyday practicality. They did not sell their quilts, although Mrs. Gilbert (Mary) Borders sometimes quilted for outsiders for a fee. All gave many away. "I always liked to give a quilt when a family got burned out," said Mrs. Thompson, and the others agreed. They still enjoyed giving quilts as wedding and family gifts, though a typical attitude was expressed by the member who added, "But I don't generally like to part with my quilts. Seems like I put so much of myself into one." Although they do not view themselves as artists, these women take much pride in their work.

The quilt pattern in the frame was a general favorite throughout the region, and Mrs. Thompson's quilts in current use reflected her liking for other popular patterns: Fan, Flower Garden, Double T, Windmill, Improved Nine-Patch, Necktie, and appliqued Tulip and Shamrock. On a couch-type bed in the room where the quilting proceeded was a Friendship Quilt to which twenty of her friends had each contributed a block, "some from as far away as Illinois," and the club had quilted it for one of her birthdays. The pattern is a big hexagon filled out to make a star. She also treasured a Postage Stamp quilt in a rectangular variation of Around the World pattern because it had been given to her by a childhood friend, Dixie Lee of Butler County, who has a flair for achieving beautiful color harmony in this pattern. "Dixie doesn't quilt—she just pieces. She gave it to me if I would quilt it, and I did," she explained. "I like to quilt. It's something to do. I don't know how to sit down and be still. We just go on making quilts because we enjoy it. When we're together we don't even realize we're working." She had quilted since early childhood, when she learned from a demanding teacher, her grandmother, who started her on a Lone Star. She could not begin to estimate how many quilts she had made in her life.

The Good Neighbor Quilting Club is far from unique in the 1970s. All across Kentucky are similar groups of social quilters who love their craft and its products. Billy Reed in his April 14, 1975, feature article in the Louisville *Courier-Journal* described a visit with an eastern Kentucky quilter who testified to the current vitality of her church quilting group. Aunt Lily Ison, eighty-one, told of meeting every Tuesday at the Marshall's Branch Freewill Baptist Church in Letcher County with a group of younger members to make quilts to sell for the church's benefit. Similar groups at that time were meeting regularly in many communities of western and central as well as eastern Kentucky. Mrs. Ison reported that her group made five or six quilts a month, enough to net about six hundred dollars a year for their church.

A group of Butler County quilters were meeting each Tuesday evening, mainly to piece their quilts, in the public library in Morgantown. An impressive display of their handiwork appeared there as part of the town's Bicentennial celebration, including one quilt that seemed especially appropriate for the occasion, outline maps of the states arranged in small blocks around a larger central square bearing the title of Woody Guthrie's song "This Land Is My Land" and the name of the maker, "Flossie Gooddall, Morgantown, Kentucky, 1972."

Some quilters of the 1970s view the bee as a past custom. Mrs. R. S. Giles of Campbellsville said, "There used to be fifteen or even more women invited to come in and make a quilt. The lady that wanted the quilt would cook dinner. . . . They were a lot of fun, but people don't do that kind of thing anymore." Mrs. P. M. Vincent of Central City recalled that she and her friends used to save the top of a favorite quilt for a quilting party. "We would do this so we could announce our plans to be married or sometimes the expectancy of a new baby." The quilting bee then filled a social need for the women, who had little time for social activities unless they were to provide necessities or "for a good cause," such as making

9

money for the church. In some communities the bees may be a past custom, but the evidence is overwhelming that they persist in every part of Kentucky.

Family Quilters

In the Jonesville Community of Hart County, Mrs. Joe Ed (Annie) Chelf learned about mid-century that some of the many tourists visiting the nearby Lincoln shrines, even before the National Park Service took them over, would eagerly buy handmade dolls and quilts. By 1975 she estimated that she had sold more than two hundred quilts in the Grandmother's Flower Garden pattern and, among others, Log Cabin quilts in several variations, the Drunkard's Path and other patterns made from its two simple shapes of a quarter-circle and its matrix, and Indian Wedding Ring and related swastika designs. She had an Oriental Poppy appliqued quilt (Plate 5) on which she had lavished so much time and careful workmanship that she had placed on it a price tag of one thousand dollars.

In retirement her husband became interested in this busy activity and entered it in his own way. He chose to specialize in making by machine quilts in Around the World and other geometric patterns such as Ocean Waves (Fig. 2), using somewhat larger pieces than do most hand quilters. He priced his quilts at about one-fourth the amount the women of the family charged for their hand-made ones. Yes, "women," for Mrs. Chelf taught interested younger women in the family and neighborhood the craft at which she was so skilled. Some of the other men followed Mr. Chelf's example to supply the steady market for Around the World quilts. The women specialized in the Flower Garden, a hexagon pattern which could be endlessly varied by color combinations.

Quilt-making for the Chelfs and their associates was profitable, but that alone did not keep the neat sign "Quilts and Dolls" on the lawn in front of their white

Figure 2. Joe Ed Chelf quilts an Ocean Waves pattern by machine. Jonesville, 1975.

house in that crossroads community. They all delighted in creating the colorful range of patterns, making Jonesville known beyond the boundaries of Kentucky for the artistic dolls and quilts available there. The quilters ranged in age from the thirties to the eighties. They also varied in their pattern preferences. Mrs. Chelf liked to copy patterns from old quilts, and treasured a quilt in the Tulip Basket pattern made in her family about 1870 from homespun thread, homegrown cotton filler, and hand-woven cloth. Tulips symbolized love for generations of brides, and early quilters often exerted their most artistic efforts on Tulip quilts. Sometimes they repeated the tulip motif in the quilting of the white areas, as in a quilt of the same period as Mrs. Chelf's in the Kentucky Museum.

Mrs. Chelf was as innovative in quilting designs as she was in piecing and appliqued work. Her controlling principle in both was to approach as nearly as possible the quality and designs of heirloom quilts she admired.

Feathers, wreaths, scrolls, floral designs, and quilting by the piece presented no more problems for her than did the overall designs of diamonds, checks, diagonals (bias lines), or shells. Border designs might be different from the quilting in the blocks but were always harmonious. Her Oriental Poppy and Rob Peter and Pay Paul (Fig. 11) illustrate the precision of her quilting. "The more quilting I can put on it, the better I like it," she said.

Mrs. Chelf used a special paring knife in preference to pencil or chalk for marking quilting designs. It was sharp enough to leave an impression but not sharp enough to damage the fabric. This kept the pure white background she often preferred at the peak of snowy perfection.

In this same small community, Mr. James Lobb had a choice small collection of older quilts, demonstrating that artistic quilting in that area was not limited to the Chelfs or to recent efforts. Among his quilts, all made by two sisters, Elizabeth Willin and Victoria Willin Graham, are the still-popular Clay's Choice, Diamond Field, Irish Chain, and Ocean Waves.

Jonesville illustrates a phenomenon that could be multiplied many times over, that of the interplay between old and new. Late-twentieth-century quilters are copying century-old patterns in contemporary materials for an active market in the mainstream of popular culture.

Arizona Martin of Bowling Green led another successful family group of quilters. Although daughter, daughter-in-law, granddaughters, and nieces often worked at regular jobs, it sometimes happened that four generations were gathered around Mrs. Martin's quilting frame. All were skilled with their needles and all took pride in their work. "We do our good quilts on our fingers," said granddaughter Myra Bumpus, Mrs. Martin's most steady assistant, "and we can't keep up with the demand for them." Myra sometimes used the more portable hoops for patterns that permitted her to work by the piece, but she and all the other members of her family preferred the tightly stretched quilt in the

Figure 3. Arizona Martin and granddaughter Myra Bumpus quilt an Improved Nine-Patch, one reach exposed. 1971.

frame, and Arizona Martin used nothing else. Myra sometimes tacked everyday quilts, and occasionally pieced one on the sewing machine, but even she preferred for her own use and for sale the handmade ones. They sometimes quilted tops others had pieced, but since their large family could keep a steady supply of scrap material coming in, they found it more profitable to make from start to finish the quilts they offered for sale.

When a local television show in 1971 had need of quilters who would not be camera shy, Arizona and Myra seated themselves comfortably at the frame to work on an Improved Nine-Patch and unself-consciously explained what they were doing as the cameras zoomed in (Fig. 3). Arizona reminisced about earlier years when she had lived on a farm near Hadley with "two everlasting springs" and led a more self-sufficient life: "We raised our own cotton and ginned it ourselves with a little wooden gin my husband had made. I carded it to make it fluffy, and I liked it better than anything we can buy now." The Martins had, however, learned to enjoy working with the new dacron and polyester synthetic fillers that were easy to sew through and did not mat when the quilts were washed, as they intended their colorfast quilts to be. Even best quilts for the Martins, as for the Good Neighbors, were functional, no matter how beautiful.

The Chelfs and the Martins, like the Good Neighbors, are representative. Such quilters are found elsewhere in Kentucky, as evidenced by media presentations, museum holdings, and the Western Kentucky University Folklore and Folklife Collection.

The Lone Quilter

In 1975 Mae Threlkeld Young lived on Clifty Hollow Road in Warren County. Her home was the saddlebag house (half log, half frame) that she and her husband had come to in 1918. Born on the Green River not far from there in 1891, she had pieced her first Nine-Patch blocks at the age of six. She pieced on a Chipyard quilt top while she sat at her husband's bedside during his terminal illness in 1974, and when she completed that king-size masterpiece in 1975, she cut out the pieces for another just like it.

On a typical day, Mae arranged herself near a Warm Morning heating stove between an antique bed and a television set. Her sewing rocker had its back to the bed so that she could face the television and a window looking out onto the front porch. On a second rocker at her left she arranged her materials—scissors, pincushion, a shoebox full of tiny cloth squares neatly segregated according to color, and the cardboard patterns she used when she cut the pieces. Her pincushion held several threaded needles. She threaded them all at once so that she wouldn't have to stop sewing to thread a needle when one gave out.

She did all her piecing "on her fingers," making neat,

even stitches to assemble the squares into colorful blocks about six by six inches. She used no template for this assembly, for long practice had given her an unerring sense of proportion. That same long practice guided her selection of colors to give their arrangement a pleasing effect both in the individual block and in the whole quilt top. When she accumulated enough blocks to make a change of pace worthwhile she sewed them together into a strip. Here some problems had to be solved. The blocks had to be put together in such a way that no two pieces of the same color came too close together. Sometimes she took the strip apart and started again if the subtle harmony of repeated hues did not suit her. As the strips accumulated, they too were sewn together, and as the weeks passed, a six-inch strip the length of the whole quilt doubled to become twelve inches wide, then eighteen, then twenty-four, and so on until the full width of a quilt was achieved.

The king-size Chipyard she completed in 1975 contained 14,400 one-inch pieces put together, in her typical six-inch block formation, with approximately 150,000 stitches. (A similar Chipyard, made in the 1960s, is shown in Plate 2.) Each piece had enough edge turned under to reduce its one-inch-square dimensions to about five-eighths of an inch showing on the finished block. These spots of color, each about the size of one's thumbnail, were not randomly distributed. Mae had been keenly conscious of texture, color, and overall effect throughout the process, demonstrating a strong feeling for good design even though she did not verbalize it. Her favorite Chipyard (Fig. 4), done when she was a young woman in her less customary rectangular whole-quilt arrangement (known by some other quilters as Around the World or Postage Stamp) had an equal number of pieces and stitches.

Each of those thousands of stitches was made with unhurried deliberation, with frequent pauses for a glance out the window at the bird feeder (patronized mostly by

Figure 4. Mae Young displays her most treasured Chipyard quilt in the arrangement many Kentucky quilters call Around the World and others call Postage Stamp. It was pieced and quilted in the 1920s.

squirrels) or the infrequent traffic on the country road. Occasionally she gave a moment's attention to the largely unattended "story" on her television set. She interrupted her sewing from time to time to attend to domestic chores—feeding the dog, cooking, tending the fire. If she talked to visitors she generally continued to ply her needle, for it was a pleasant task that had become almost automatic.

Mae Young was proud of her work in textiles. She liked to recall spinning and weaving in her youth. She had raised flax for linen and had washed and dyed the home-sheared wool of sheep raised on the farm. She recalled that weaving was on the decline in her community even when she married, so much so that she and Charley decided to abandon the loom when they moved into the small house that was to be their lifelong home. She still prized a handwoven coverlet made for her by her grandmother in a pattern she called The Soldiers' March to the Sea, and kept it put away as a reminder of her family traditions.

Without too much persuasion Mae would show the pieced tops stored in a large chest in her bedroom. Why did she have so many unquilted tops? Because she had stopped quilting many years before when her declining stamina and agility made the work strenuous. As she unloaded the chest her visitor was treated to a veritable catalog of pieced quilt patterns: Snake Trail, Thomas Jefferson, Double T, Seven Stars, Tumbling Blocks, Turkey Tracks, Jacob's Ladder, Lone Star, Drunkard's Path, Wonder of the World, Log Cabin (in Sunshine and Shade, Barn Raising, and other variations), Nine-Patch, and many others. Each one called up memories. Charley had brought the dress these pieces came from on one of his return trips by riverboat from Evansville. Here were scraps a neighbor had given her in exchange for some of hers. She recognized yet another top that she had been working on when she and Charley had to bring orphan lambs into the kitchen. Another one she adapted from a jigsaw puzzle she had seen at Sears Roebuck and had Charley cut the templates from wood. Several of the patterns were from family or neighborhood tradition. Neighbors exchanged patterns (templates) of thin cardboard as well as blocks showing favorite designs. Yet others she had copied from pictures in newspaper or farm magazine advertisements, saving the cost of the pattern, which in the 1930s was over a dollar each. She had done appliques but much preferred the pieced designs.

Mae did not need the quilt tops, but she was not eager to part with them either, for reminders of all kinds of experiences over the years were worked into those designs stored in the big chest. As she had become more sedentary, she had reduced her repertory, cutting off quilting first, then narrowing down to a variation on a single pattern which she could handle without confusion. Each Chipyard, she had announced, would be her last, but creating beautiful objects had become too much a habit for her to break easily. Each time she completed one, she was restless until she settled down to another accumulation of brightly colored one-inch squares. Since her scrap box had been well stocked over the years, she could rationalize beginning yet another new top with the explanation, "I have plenty of material on hand to make another one." For her Chipyard tops she liked the tiny, almost invisible printed patterns in percale and broadcloth that resemble the early calicos, yet she wasted nothing.

In the early years of her marriage, "before the county road came," when quilts were by far the most economical bedcovers available in her out-of-the-way rural community, she even opened up Charley's small tobacco sacks of "brown domestic," or unbleached muslin. They were just the right size to dye and make what local quilters have always called a Brick quilt, since the pieces worked into the quilt top look about the shape and size of bricks in a wall. This was, of course, considered an everyday quilt, in the same category as the String quilt, and was the only one in Mae's collection that she had pieced by machine. She had dyed half of the pieces bright yellow and left the other half in their natural color for contrast.

Mae Young illustrates the "lone quilter" tradition to which literally thousands of Kentucky women have belonged—those who lived far apart or were temperamentally less gregarious than those who preferred to work in groups. They have been at work for generations in all parts of Kentucky from the mountains to the Purchase, each one influenced by her own family and her ties with the community, and, through printed media, radio, and television, influenced by the mainstream of American popular culture. A few are too "particular" about their proud craftsmanship to be satisfied with group production; others are seldom free to be away from home. Their hanging frames may be pulled up against the ceiling of the most comfortable room in the house most of the year, to be pulled down during the winter when little outdoor work is needed.

Each of the lone quilters has her favorite patterns for piecing or applique; each has her favorite method of quilting. Even the methods of binding differ. Some like to use a separate binding of bias tape in a contrasting color. Others like to turn the top over onto the backing. Still others like to turn the backing over onto the top, sewing it down with nearly invisible stitches. The border may be a straight edge or may have scallops, swags (large scallops), or points.

The great majority of these quilters prefer not to make a big project of their work but to pick it up as they have the time. The old-time quilters are seldom oriented to the commercial possibilities of their craft. They do a thing they can do well—for the usefulness of the product, as a way to conserve scraps, and for the varied possibilities for using what they have to make something "pretty."

In Mae Young's quilting are discernible many of the generalizations that apply to the craft wherever it appears. Quilt-making has tenuous connections with weaving in terms of domestic crafts and utility. Both crafts have had some association with frugality and ingenuity. Intermingled as they are with other domestic activities, the individual products are bound up with the individual maker's history, and taken as a whole they reflect the history of the Commonwealth. Always apparent is the striving for effect, reflecting the maker's need for beauty in her surroundings.

2

FRUGALITY AND SELF-SUFFICIENCY

Both piecework and quilting are activities that reach too far back into history to establish their beginnings. It seems reasonable to assume that piecework began as a strictly utilitarian salvage activity—sewing together useless scraps to make a piece of cloth large enough to be useful in some way. Quilting, whether by sewing through a cloth sandwich with continuous seams or by some variation of tacking, is a way of making the filler stay in place. It is utilitarian and does not necessarily have anything to do with piecing. The two activities, however, would inevitably come together for making bedcovers at an early date, for the pieced top serves better in that function than it does as material for clothing.

Functional as the pieced and quilted bedcover must have been in the beginning, the infinite ways in which the scraps could be arranged for pleasing effects would suggest deliberate patterning, and the large expanse of top to be made fast to the other two layers would invite experimentation with techniques and patterning in the quilting. As this tradition of creativity grew, the aesthetic appeal began to provide its own motivation, displacing to some degree mere physical comfort as the quilter's sole consideration. For some quilters, striving for effect gradually diminished the salvage nature of the craft. In some instances the highly artistic or elaborately contrived quilt has, indeed, gone all the way to such extravagance in material and labor that one hesitates to put it to any of the practical uses ordinarily associated with quilts. Such artwork becomes an heirloom for several generations and then possibly a museum piece. In a later chapter some of these will be described in detail.

These two contrasting themes, frugality and extravagance, were clearly established in Europe even before Colonial times in America. They continue today and are manifested in any collection of Kentucky quilts.

An interesting example of the old-timer's habitual concern for the most basic human needs came up when Mae Young learned about a family moving into the neighborhood in midwinter. She wondered if they had enough warm bedcovers and offered to send some if they were needed. Another woman, harking back to an earlier time, recalled that her mother, Mrs. Eli Meador, had always sent quilts to unfortunate families whose homes had been destroyed by fire.

Many of the quilts piled high over a sleeper in a chilly upstairs bedroom were made strictly for warmth. Large squares of wool salvaged from men's suits, wool skirts, and other cast-off clothing were pieced together for a top, then tacked with ample filler to an outing flannel backing. This technique produced the heaviest, warmest, and usually the least attractive of the utilitarian quilts. It was also the least demanding in terms of both time and skill with needle and thread. One quilt in current use was made a generation ago by the owner's father and sister, who worked in an Evansville, Indiana, furniture factory. It is made of heavy upholstery material salvaged at the factory and tacked without filler to an outing flannel backing. Even small children could help tie knots in the tacking yarn while such a quilt was in the frame.

Tacking, known elsewhere variously as tying or knotting, receives little attention now but figures prominently in the memories of many who grew up sleeping under quilts. Woolen quilts, old quilts being recovered, quilts of heavy materials, and quilts for any reason considered unsuitable for quilting designs are stretched in a frame, basted or pinned, and marked with straight intersecting lines at right angles. Heavy yarn, twine, or embroidery floss is threaded through a rather large needle and pulled through to leave large loops on the top. The loops are then cut and tied in square knots and later trimmed to even lengths, adding a decorative effect to these most humble quilts. Unless an older quilt is getting a reprieve from the ragbag, this type of bedcover often has no filler, and outing, denim, or upholstery fabric may be used for the lining.

Some do not consider this process quilting at all. Mrs. Earl (Zena) Thomas of Bowling Green says, "I never quilted. I always tacked mine." She did not tie knots but at regular intervals secured her heavy stitching with a backstitch. Mrs. Joe (Bonnie) Willis, who reserves this technique for covering an old quilt, secures her stitching at intervals with an ornamental lazy-daisy stitch. Mrs. Elzie (Ellen) Barrow uses a cross-stitch. A tacked quilt is usually called a "comfort." All quilters interviewed in the region considered such quilts strictly utilitarian, but many who have won local recognition for their "good quilts" have also made comforts.

Frontier conditions in early times made cloth enough of a luxury to prompt conservation. No scrap of cloth was wasted. This may partially account for the popularity of such patterns as Snake Trail and Double Wedding Ring, which consume many very small scraps. Even though frontier conditions are long gone, the habit of frugality remains. Contemporary Kentucky quilters reflect it in a variety of interesting ways.

Mae Young's use of her husband's empty tobacco sacks was part of a widespread practice. Mrs. Meador, her

Figure 5. Quilt lining made of Acme Feed sacks. The neat quilting pattern follows the block design of the top. Mrs. Ben Harrison, Bee Spring, Edmonson County.

neighbor, also used them. Miss Evelyn Fuqua reports that she used nine hundred tobacco sacks in one quilt. The custom of asking the men to save these little pieces of unbleached muslin has been reported widely.

The tobacco sack salvage has its analogue in the use of feed sacks for backing. Some feed sacks come in colorful prints as an added attraction for the home seamstress. Before this trend, however, feed sacks with the label showing were used for utility quilts. Mrs. Ben Harrison of Edmonson County happily showed the illustrated example of "Acme" labels on the backing of one of her quilts (Fig. 5). She had another reversible quilt made entirely of patterned feed sacks. She laughed at its coarseness but boasted of its durability and usefulness on a bed occupied by male kinsmen who "dropped in" during hunting or harvest season. She also showed a reversible quilt made entirely from salvaged sugar sacks and two quilts filled with wool sheared and carded on her farm in 1945. Among the patterns she displayed were Dove at the

Window, Star, and Sunshine and Shade. It was Mrs. Harrison, too, who recalled another frugal trait—permitting the children to make their own thread from ravelings.

For the urban dweller who does not smoke granulated tobacco or buy stock feed, there are other sources of scrap cloth, both for piecework and for backing. Cast-off clothing saved by family, friends, and neighbors is a standard source. No matter how worn the garment, it is likely to furnish a few scraps of relatively unworn material. If other sources fail, the nearby thrift store can provide.

Gracie Sanders during the winter of 1975 was living alone in a large old-fashioned house in Hartford, Kentucky. The high-ceilinged old rooms had many memories for her but were hard to heat in the winter. Gracie needed warm quilts, and since her children and grandchildren came often she needed plenty of them. She tended to concentrate, both from current needs and from the habit of a lifetime, on warmth as first priority in a quilt. She pieced her tops at odd hours, then set up the quilting frame to finish them in the winter, quilting the lighter-weight cottons and tacking the heavier woolens. She was proud of her ingenuity in making pretty quilts from economical materials, some given to her by family, friends, and neighbors. A sister in Louisville provided scraps from a drapery factory. Gracie also found a satisfactory source of warm, inexpensive materials in her local Goodwill Industries store. She could buy good strong cloth in used suits and dresses, rip out the seams, wash the material, and cut out quilt pieces. One of the quilts from this source was made entirely from used corduroy garments (Fig. 6). Because Gracie was too frugal to waste good material, some of the quilt pieces show the outline of a pocket that has been carefully removed or a side placket that has been ripped open and pressed flat. In spite of this stress on frugal utility, the quilt shows the distribution of red and blue pieces among the brown and duller shades

Figure 6. Detail of a utility quilt made of used corduroy clothing (note outline of ripped-off pocket at center), tacked without filler to a heavy lining of upholstery scraps. Gracie Sanders, Hartford, 1974. Author's collection.

to achieve a warm glow of cheerful color. Because she had to pay cash for filler, Gracie omitted it in the heavy quilts. She had been pleased to have her "nicer" quilts admired and sought after by enthusiasts as far away as Louisville and Lexington.

Factory salvage finds its way to quilters by various routes. One factory in Bowling Green bundles up its scraps and permits an employee to buy a large bundle at a bargain price. Some bundles then find their way to members of the family or friends who can use them. A clothing factory in Morgantown simply sends scraps to the city dump. "You can see all kinds of well-off people in good cars out there picking it over," said one observant resident. These well-off salvage hunters are not necessarily penurious. An enthusiastic quilter, whatever her station in society, is always on the lookout for new sources and new kinds of material.

"It's from the Derby," a young woman remarked as soon as she saw a newly pieced quilt top. She was using the familiar local reference to an underwear factory in Bowling Green. Scraps from this source, good quality broadcloth stripes and figure prints, are easy to recognize even after they have been pieced into a quilt. One suburban housewife in a "good neighborhood" was apologetic for using this source but also praised the tough quality of the materials for everyday quilts.

Although the continuous traditions are strong and appear at first examination to be rather static, a closer look reveals that even the most conservative quilters exchange information about pattern variations and materials. It is not surprising, then, to discover enthusiastic experimentation with double-knit scraps. Some quilters like Sidney Chapman of Butler County express their delight in the ease with which double-knit works up and the ease of laundering a double-knit quilt with dacron filler and drip-dry lining. Others, like Sidney's friend Dixie Lee, spurn the new fabric because "it won't lay flat." The principal reason for this experimentation seems to be frugality. Nothing should go to waste and the clothing factory is now making double-knit scraps available in quantity.

A never-failing source for Crazy Quilt material is the endless variety found in discarded neckties. A man's tie wears very little, but styles change and surplus ties accumulate. One necktie ripped open and pressed flat contains a substantial piece of good material, yet it is too small for any other use. Piecing necktie material into quilts or throws is a perfect example of salvage art. This material is usually meant to be decorative rather than strong; often it has the kind of fragility found in pretty ribbons, brocades, velvet, and dimity—all of which have been used in Crazy Quilt designs and none of which has lasting qualities.

One example of self-defeating frugality is the case of the quilt top that came apart. A rural woman who regularly pieces attractive tops for herself and her relatives discovered the current urban revival of interest in traditional quilting and decided to make some tops for sale. She cut her pieces from lightweight gingham scraps and tried to get maximum use from them by stitching quite close to the edge. Her quilt tops were beautiful, reflecting a fine eye for color combinations, but the first purchaser returned the top because it started pulling apart before it could be set up in the frame.

A very popular design for using up miscellaneous cloth scraps is the String quilt. No quilter interviewed considered a String quilt one of her show pieces, yet some are quite beautiful. "It's just an old String quilt," said one quilter, giving a typical response to an inquiry about a quilt using irregular shapes and sizes of brightly colored prints and solids. They had been sewed onto a square newspaper pattern with ends protruding around the edges at random. The squares were trimmed to the paper pattern dimensions and then "set up," first by sewing them into strips and then by combining the strips, with a narrow strip of white or contrasting color to form a frame for each block. Many of these quilts are tacked instead of quilted because they are lightly valued and the amount of time, thread, and energy used in fancy quilting would be considered a waste.

The theme of frugality and utility carries on through the life of a quilt. After it becomes faded and ragged from years of regular use and occasional laundering it finds its way to the bedsprings as a protective pad, to the seat of the pickup truck, to the doghouse, or to the tobacco barn. A common use in the days when the upstairs of a badly chinked log house was likely to be drafty was reminiscent of the use of medieval tapestries—as wall hangings to cut down drafts and provide an illusion, at least, of coziness.

Perhaps the most remarkable example of the quilter's pioneer attitude toward frugal self-sufficiency is the persistence into the 1970s of home-grown, home-ginned, home-carded cotton for quilt filler. Mrs. Melissa Steen-berger, a Barren County quilter, raised her own cotton and processed it for quilts. She said in a 1974 interview for the Western Kentucky University Folklore and Folk-life Collection that she had plenty of cotton stored in the attic to supply her needs for some time. Mrs. Ethel Vaughan of Marion recalled in 1974 that she had always planted her cotton on the first day of May. Mrs. Youree (Hattie Willis) Howell said in March 1976 that she would have to buy stuffing for her next quilt, a thing she had never had to do before. Her family, the Willises of Allen County, had for generations raised, ginned, and carded their own cotton for quilt-making. Although few quilters still raise their own cotton, many recall it and uniformly state their preference for the quality of the home-processed filler.

The homemade cotton gin employs two small wooden rollers set up like a clothes wringer and operated by hand cranks. The rollers squeeze the seed out of the raw cotton fibers after the fibers have been warmed. Mae Young recalls that her brother made such a gin by using "barn boards and two chair rounds for rollers." Both the cotton gins and the cotton cards are common mementos of this activity.

Self-sufficiency is not confined to materials for the quilts themselves; it extends to quilting equipment. Everyday people working at this everyday craft have made hundreds of minor adaptations. Their little inventions get passed around and further improved upon. Ordinarily quilting frames are homemade. The two general types are hanging frames and trestle, or standing, frames. The hanging frame is suspended from the ceiling, swinging freely on four cords attached to hooks screwed into the ceiling, one for each corner. The trestle frame is supported from below by some device similar to a sawhorse. The choice seems to depend on individual preference and convenience. The trestle frame has the advantage of being movable from storage to a working area or from one working area to another. The hanging frame can be pulled up out of the way to clear the area for other activities without disturbing the unfinished work. It takes only a minute or two to lower the whole assembly, pull up a chair, and resume work. Since it is free swinging, it does not provide as stable a work surface as a trestle frame does, but in a small house it can be an advantage in that one can crowd past the fully extended frame by pushing it aside.

Trestle frames come in many shapes, generally being about as long as a carpenter's sawhorse. The height is critical in that the quilt top must be low enough to provide a good work surface, high enough to permit the quilter to pull a chair up to the edge and reach across the top for about two feet—about the limit of a comfortable "reach." The two crossrails, somewhat longer than the conventional width of a quilt, must be substantial enough to hold the weight of the extended quilt without sagging, light enough to assemble and manipulate conveniently. Pieces of seasoned oak about one by two inches in cross-section are suitable. These pieces have holes about an eighth of an inch in diameter drilled through them at short intervals for "pinning" the rails to the horses (sometimes loosely with a large nail). A more elaborate arrangement is to use rails with a square cross-section and horses with corresponding notches cut into their top surfaces so that the rails inserted into them are held firmly in place a reach apart. A still more elaborate arrangement is to have the near (to the quilter) rail cut to a circular cross-section near both ends so that it can fit into semicircular slots on the trestle, and to lock it in place with a ratchet arrangement so that it can rotate in one direction.

Putting the quilt into the frame must be done carefully. The lining must be stretched fully on the floor and weighted at the corners while the two ends are pinned or whipstitched with coarse thread or twine to narrow strips of strong cloth tacked to the two rails of the frame. Next the cotton or polyester "batting" is stretched evenly over

29

the lining, reaching almost to the edges, the top is laid over it, and the three layers are pinned or basted together. Finally the whole quilt must be wound carefully and tightly around one side of the frame toward the top, leaving only a single reach exposed. The rolled-up section on the fixed rail is then locked in place and the near end is ready for fastening to the near rail. The quilt is pinned at the sides to strips of cloth wrapped around the sawhorses. Pins are preferable to stitching for this, since they must be removed and reinserted as the quilting progresses. When one reach has been fully quilted, the next unfinished area is released from the far rail, the finished work is rolled under, the new work is adjusted to be even and tight, and quilting proceeds.

Setting a quilt into a hanging frame is a similar process. The four sides of the hanging frame are similar to the two rails used on the trestle frame. Holes bored through them at intervals make them adjustable in length at all four corners. A nail or a wooden pin pushed through holes matched up at a corner locks it. Since the hanging frame does not have the limitation imposed by supporting structures, the quilt can be fastened into the frame fully exposed. The same coarse thread or twine is pulled through the edge of the quilt and around a rail in widely separated loops. Again, as a reach is finished it is rolled under, bringing a new work surface within reach of the quilter.

A variation of the hanging frame employs the same four rails pinned at the corners, but it is supported at each corner by a chair, stool, or any other piece of suitable furniture. These supports can be moved closer together as the corners are loosened to roll up a finished reach, thus gradually diminishing the size, from the quilt fully exposed at the beginning to the narrow strip of the last reach.

Either the hanging or the trestle frame consumes space in the room while it is being used. The lone quilter who finds such a device inconvenient can use a pair of hoops

30

similar to the conventional embroidery hoops except for size. These round or oval quilting hoops are ordinarily purchased rather than homemade. Some are attached to a low adjustable stand, the type Wilma Lee uses. They are large enough to hold a section of quilt, small enough for portable lap work. Mrs. Lee has used her hoop for quilts from crib size to king size. She prefers patterns that can be quilted by the piece or the block, such as Dresden Plate or Wedding Ring. Eutha Clark saved her mother's quilting hoops, not because they were remarkably good but because they were a reminder of Mrs. Meador's ingenuity and self-sufficiency. They were two discarded barrel hoops covered with cloth, one enough larger than the other to make a tight fit with quilt interposed.

The opposite extremes of frugality and extravagance can be seen in the quilt-making of any period. The well-to-do could indulge their taste for style and luxury, while the hard-working yeomen did their best with what they had. This contrast has held true right up to the present. Whether motivated by necessity or by inclination, however, every quilt-maker has had an opportunity to display her skill and imagination. A Star quilt (Fig. 7) in soft blue-striped homespun cotton illustrates this well. The quilt has a backing of coarsely woven natural linen. Both the cotton and the linen were grown on the farm where the quilt was made. A small eight-pointed star at the center of the quilt is the point of convergence for strips of blue-striped material which form the four large quadrants. (This arrangement of the quilt top into four yard-square blocks is rare in Kentucky collections, its scarcity seeming to support Ruth Finley's statement in *Old Patchwork Quilts and the Women Who Made Them* that the type was out of style in America before 1850.) An eight-point star appears in each of the four squares, each star containing seventy-two small diamond pieces so arranged that the stripes in the material give the illusion of a turning movement. It shows some characteristics of

Figure 7. One-fourth of a blue and white Star quilt in coarse cotton with a homespun lining. Nancy Bird Brooks, Hart County, 1813. Kentucky Museum.

Broken Star (Dutch Rose), Double T, and Tumbling Blocks. Like so many geometric patterns, it creates optical illusions for the viewer as the eyes move to different focal points.

This quilt has the mellow charm of a useful object made attractive by people in an era of make-do necessity. Nancy Bird Brooks, mother of W. H. Owen of Hart County, made this quilt in 1813. It belongs to the same era as the all-white quilt made by Rebecca Washington in Logan County (Figs. 42–44), a quilt which evokes a more leisurely life-style in a wealthier household. In both cases self-sufficiency is reflected in the home production of some of the materials, and in both cases the quilters created an attractive original expression of their craft.

One can find many quilts which do not express frugality, but every quilt to some degree reflects the theme of self-sufficiency, for the quilter, whatever her station, whatever her design, combines her materials, her skills, and her plan to create a useful object where there was none before.

3

THEIR INFINITE VARIETY

You HAVE TO HAVE a little artist about you," a quilter
said, explaining the impulse that has kept quilters
piecing and quilting bedcovers by hand in an era of
readily available and relatively inexpensive machine-
made blankets and coverlets. To a tradition-oriented
person, as so many native Kentuckians are, sleeping
under a "right pretty quilt" made by a member of his
family or a neighbor, especially if it is in one of the old
familiar patterns, conveys a subtle warmth involved with
appreciation of continuity in his cultural heritage.
Beauty, it is true, is in the eye of the beholder, and the
patchwork quilt, although Kentucky quilters have never
ceased to make it, has been many times in and out of
fashion. Some repertories show the quilter's preference
for neat, small geometric designs against a background of
stark white, others for large patterns of bold color. Some
are made simply with utility in mind, others with such
intricate complexities that only the most skilled needle-
woman can rise to the challenge. The word art suggests
imagination and an intent to produce an object that goes
beyond utility, no matter how functional it may be. Many
will prefer the word craft for the mainstream of Kentucky
quilting, past and present. Yet as skeptics look at a sampling of quilts they are likely to grant that the most

practical-minded quilter has a little artist about her.

Aside from their numbers, Kentucky quilters can make few claims to distinction. Their techniques and patterns on the whole demonstrate ingenious adaptations rather than unique conceptions. Most of them have tried piecing, applique, and at least one novelty quilt, and each quilter tends to have preferences in materials and patterns. Kentucky quilters have followed the mainstream in America by preferring block organization rather than large overall designs. Jonathan Holstein in *The Pieced Quilt* viewed this preference as a logical and functional approach when fast and economical quilt-making was a pioneer necessity: "The block-style pieced technique in which pieces are cut into largely geometric, straight-edged forms was itself the most efficient method, in terms of both time and material, for using surplus fabric and joining it together" [p. 50].

For readers who are not quilters the vocabulary of the craft can be confusing. The language varies both regionally and historically. The word patch, for example, to some is synonymous with piece; to others it applies only to appliqued work in which one piece is superimposed on another; to still others it occurs only in reference to two universally known families of quilt patterns, the Four-Patch and the Nine-Patch. In this book, following the practice of quilters in south-central Kentucky, the word patch will be used only in the context of Four-Patch and Nine-Patch. It should be noted, however, that "four-patch" and "nine-patch" have their special application in any discussion of quilt-making, since they relate to the primary division of a block into pieces. The term block refers to a design unit of any size, most often a square, usually made of smaller pieces of various shapes. Beginning quilters have favored the fundamental Four-Patch or the fundamental Nine-Patch, both of which involve only one basic shape—the square—for both pieces and blocks. A typical Kentucky quilter began as Mae Young and

Arizona Martin did, by piecing blocks for one of these in early childhood.

An experienced quilter can look closely at a quilt or even at a picture of one, analyze the structure into blocks and a block into pieces. Then she can take a square of cloth the size of the block she desires to make, fold it, and cut the needed pattern shapes for templates. She must, of course, have in mind or on paper a diagram of their arrangement and the number needed. Annie Chelf laughs at the labor she expended to "take off" a complicated pattern from a picture, only to discover the ready-made pattern later on. And Mae Young, who found she had lost her pattern for Jacob's Ladder when she got ready to make another one, said, "It won't be hard to cut another. It's just squares and half-squares." She had in her memory the structure of the block.

Most quilters keep the pattern templates of cardboard (sandpaper in recent years) or some other durable material and pass them around among their fellow quilters during their lifetimes. The Kentucky Museum has a file of templates, those for each pattern in a separate brown envelope. The quilter needs for most patterns a diagram either in her mind or on paper indicating the number of pieces to cut for each shape (or color variation within the shape) and showing the arrangement of pieces into blocks and of blocks into a whole top. The small blocks of ancient and ever-popular Windmill (also called Pinwheel) and of Kaleidoscope form the same overall design no matter how the blocks are assembled into the square or rectangular top, but such patterns are the exception rather than the rule.

Since even the large categories of pieced, appliqued, and novelty quilts at times overlap, no attempt has been made here to place Kentucky quilts in tight categories. For convenience of discussion, however, the following organization will be loosely applied: pieced, according to structure; appliqued, according to subject; and novelty, according to the novel characteristic.

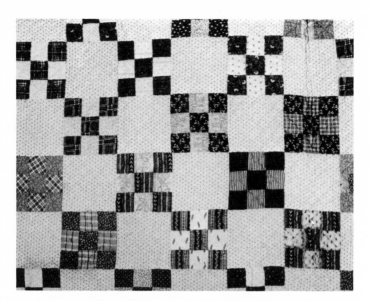

Figure 8. Section of Nine-Patch with Irish Chain effect. Ellen Kellis Huffines, Woodburn, about 1900. Kentucky Museum.

Pieced Quilts: Angular Patterns

"Strictly everyday quilts!" exclaimed Mrs. Mattie Gilley of the Wisdom Community near Glasgow, speaking of the Four-Patch and the Nine-Patch. Although Mrs. Gilley at age eighty has executed many variations on these basic block patterns, she has cared enough to preserve carefully a fundamental Four-Patch made long ago by her grandmother. Hardly a collection, large or small, is without at least one quilt in this simple pattern of contrasting small squares.

A well-worn but finely crafted Nine-Patch in the Kentucky Museum (Fig. 8) patterns a variety of colored prints on a light pin dot background, its five-inch blocks set together in such a way that the quilt can also be viewed as a single Irish Chain, with chained squares running diagonally. Ellen Kellis Huffines of Woodburn is reported to have pieced the top when she was nine years old late in the nineteenth century. The quilting, fine and even far beyond utility, surely required a more experienced hand. A similar one of about the same vintage, a treasured possession of Harold Clark of north Warren County, has graceful long-stemmed flowers quilted in the white squares that alternate with the quilted checks of the pattern blocks. The Nine-Patch and Four-Patch have by no means always functioned as everyday quilts. Most Kentucky quilters would nonetheless agree with Mrs. Gilley.

The variations possible on the basic Four-Patch and Nine-Patch can be more clearly envisioned if one remembers the first principle of designing the quilt block. Two or more colors must be used so that the small pieces can be assembled into a design that depends on their contrasting hues. For a Four-Patch, a square of cloth should be folded in half each way, then cut into four equal smaller squares. Blocks should be so divided for each color or fabric the quilter plans to use. In the fundamental Four-Patch pattern, alternating colors or alternating dark and light pieces will be used to achieve the typical checkerboard effect. For a Nine-Patch the square will be folded into thirds each way to yield nine small squares for each color; then the small squares will be assembled with alternating colors so that the center and four corners are in contrast with the pieces in between. In either of these structures any or all of the four or nine pieces can be subdivided into smaller parts of any shape desired.

The Windmill is a good illustration of a simple variation on the basic Four-Patch block. Each of the four squares is subdivided diagonally into the type of triangles some quilters call half-squares, the four dark ones forming the vanes of the windmill. Some quilters like to elaborate this pattern, as Thala Thompson does, by further subdividing the dark triangles into two contrasting colors. Quilters who enjoy creating optical illusions with this pattern, as Mae Young does, combine the Windmill blocks without separating strips, or they alternate pattern blocks with

38

Figure 9 *(above)* Detail of Windmill. Figure 10 *(below)* Detail of Dutchman's Puzzle. Both by an unidentified Kentucky quilt-maker. Displayed in a folklore class at Western Kentucky University, 1971.

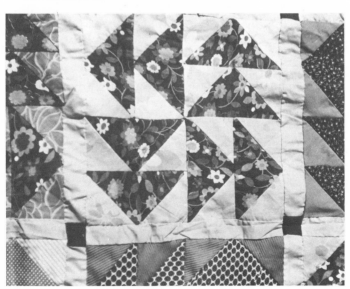

39

solid color blocks. One Kentucky quilter pieced her Windmill quilt of bright colors, combining four of a kind to form a larger block. The design is continuous, but the changing patterns of color as the larger blocks are set together provide an interesting effect (Fig. 9). The same quilter pieced a Dutchman's Puzzle (Fig. 10) in large and small triangles of multicolored materials but used narrow pastel blue strips and small red squares at the corners to define the large blocks of the pattern.

A simple variation on the Nine-Patch is Shoo Fly, in which each of the corner squares is cut diagonally in half so that the corner triangles can contrast. A popular modern variation known as Improved Nine-Patch appears to have been well established by the 1930s, when it appeared in quilting manuals. This pattern shows an elongation of the four corner pieces and the insertion of a straight-based arc to square the unit block on all sides. This arrangement creates the effect of enclosing each Nine-Patch pattern within a large circle, and also creates the optical illusion of a large four-point star in the solid-color material which separates the now starlike nine-patches (Fig. 3, Plate 2). This pattern may have been influenced by one of the variants of Rob Peter and Pay Paul (Fig. 11), also known as Orange Peel, which makes a similar use of a straight-based arc to square the block. Even when quilters in the same community make this pattern, their variations of color combinations and degree of elongation in the corners make every quilt a unique creation.

The overwhelming preference among Kentucky quilters for block patterns has some notable exceptions, one of them being the whole-quilt design often called Trip Around the World in other parts of the United States and presented here variously as Around the World, Chipyard (one style, Fig. 4), and Postage Stamp (one style). The Around the World patterns, which may be square, rectangular, or rotated forty-five degrees to give a large diamond effect, begin with a small square at the center (or several

PLATE 1. *Above:* Bicentennial quilt in Lone Star pattern. Pieced and quilted by Elizabeth Ward of Princeton, Caldwell County, 1975. Kentucky Museum. *Below:* One-fourth of an Album Quilt top. Maker and date unknown; found in the attic of Willie Price's family farmhouse by his widow, present owner Lelia Price, Hadley, Warren County.

PLATE 2. *Above:* One block of Improved Nine-Patch. Pieced and quilted by Arizona Martin and her granddaughter Myra Bumpus, Bowling Green, 1970. *Below:* Small section of Chipyard, more commonly called Postage Stamp. Pieced in blocks by Mae Young, Warren County; quilted by Ellen Barrow, Morgantown, 1970. Author's collection.

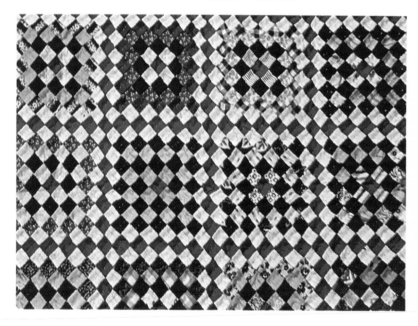

PLATE 3. *Above:* Section of quilt, elsewhere identified as Star of Chamblie. Made by Ruth Bennett Lindley of Livermore, McLean County, for donor Lenora E. Lindley, late nineteenth century. Kentucky Museum. *Below:* Section of Poplar Leaf, known also by other regional names. Pieced by Kathleen Kelly, sister of owner Sidney Chapman, Sugar Grove Community, Butler County; quilted by Wilma Lee, Butler County, about 1974.

PLATE 4. *Above:* Section of Cathedral Windows. Made by the owner, Mrs. Jack Underwood, Glasgow, contemporary. *Below:* Section of Snake Trail. Made by the owner, Mrs. Bennett Clark, Riverside, before World War II.

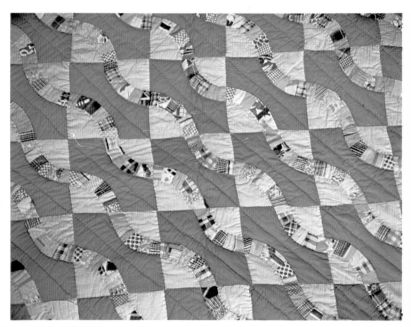

PLATE 5

One block and section of border of appliqued quilt elsewhere identified as Whig Rose. Made by Mrs. Leighton Mabram, about 1843. Donated to the Kentucky Museum by Mrs. Clarence Wahm, Bowling Green.

Above: Center of appliqued quilt elsewhere identified as Rose of Sharon variation. Probably made by the wife and sister of William Sharp, Mercer County, mid-nineteenth century. Donated to the Kentucky Museum by Hattie Funk, Bowling Green. *Left:* One pattern block (of nine) of Oriental Poppy. Made by owner Annie Chelf of Jonesville, Hart County, contemporary.

PLATE 6. *Above:* Center section of a highly organized parlor throw giving prominence to wheel of fortune and swastika motifs in both piecing and fancy stitching. Kentucky Museum. *Below:* Section of a velvet quilt elsewhere identified as Windows and Doors. Made as a Friendship Quilt, World War I era, by Mrs. Elwood Wand and owned by her son, Thomas P. Wand of Woodbury, Butler County.

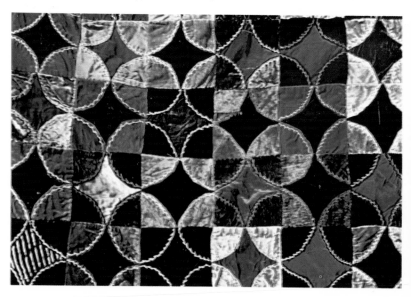

PLATE 7. *Above:* Section of a Friendship Quilt. Made by Maggie D. Williams of Ohio County in 1886-1888. Great-granddaughter Frances Hoover Loving donated it to the Kentucky Museum. *Below:* Center section of a Crazy Quilt giving prominence to Kentucky racehorse Chester Dare. Made by Annie Hines Miller, Warren County, late nineteenth century. Owned by Nina McGinnis Stone Venable, Bowling Green.

PLATE 8. Unnamed, undated quilt, a variation of Tumbling Blocks arranged to form a cross against a four-point star. Kentucky Museum.

Figure 11. Section of Rob Peter and Pay Paul (elsewhere called Orange Peel). Annie Chelf, Jonesville, contemporary.

small squares chained vertically to form the center for a rectangle) and depend on the quilter's use of color to achieve an effective design. These patterns have been popular with quilters and with collectors who enjoy their endlessly varied effects. Quilters often like to tell how many pieces they have used in a Postage Stamp quilt in this pattern. The highest numbers achieved among the quilters represented in this discussion are more than 17,000 by Bonnie Willis of Riverside and more than 14,000 by Mae Young.

More scattered but interesting are pictorial whole-quilt designs made up of small squares, possibly inspired by cross-stitch embroidery. Chloe Meador, mother of Mrs. Harold (Eutha) Clark, enjoyed making quilt-size novelty designs of squares. One was a Mule quilt, appropriate enough for a part of the state where many farmers still prefer mules to machines for some stages of crop cultivation. She laid out her design in postage stamp-size squares of dark material to achieve a remarkable likeness to a mule, and filled out the top to the desired size with unbleached muslin. The inspiration for attempting this tedious work may well have been a favorite grandson, affectionately called Mule during his boyhood. For years he used the quilt on his bed, taking pride in his grandmother's needlecraft and enjoying the novelty of the design.

Kentucky quilters have always liked Log Cabin designs, the most popular variations being Sunshine and Shade and Barn Raising. Flossie Sheriff McClure of Lexington, who in her eighth decade has given up quilting, made them in beautiful variations, her designs comparable to the most highly prized quilts of a century earlier. Naomi Deane Stuart, wife of Kentucky author Jesse Stuart, treasures a Light and Dark Log Cabin quilt his mother made of scraps from Jesse's little boy shirts and pants. Western Kentucky University English professor Charles Snow Guthrie values one made by Ada Guthrie Bryson of Burkesville, which she called Light and Dark Paths.

The Log Cabin block begins with a small square, around which rectangles of gradually increasing size build up to the full block. The object is to form a finished block which is diagonally divided into light and dark shades. Different ways of constructing the blocks and different ways of setting them together allow the quilter much room for creativity. As utility quilts in wools and cottons, as scrap quilts mixing fabrics, or as silk and velvet quilts for parlor throws or keepsakes, these are among Kentucky's most colorful and interesting quilts.

Matilda Potter Backus of Bowling Green, who was born in 1853, made her Barn Raising quilt of very narrow silk strips and varied the fabric textures in black for her dark sections. Instead of placing the half-light and half-dark blocks to run in wide diagonal paths across the quilt, as in Sunshine and Shade, she arranged them to form square or diamond paths around a fairly large central square. The effect is of larger and larger enclosures around the central square, which in Mrs. Backus's quilt is vivid magenta.

The Kentucky Museum has this and several similar Log Cabin quilts by other regional quilt-makers of the late nineteenth century—enough to demonstrate that silk Log Cabin parlor throws were as popular in some circles as were the more practical wools and cottons in others. Some quilters made both. Even ribbons and fine neckties could be worked into the designs. Mae Young, Annie Chelf, and Thala Thompson are representative of the many who have made diversified Log Cabin designs in recent years, most often of cotton.

Another possible variation was demonstrated by Blanche Carlisle Critser who, in her seventies, combined 3,480 narrow strips of cotton from clothing discarded over a generation by the children in her family to make a pattern she called Little Fingers, derived from a combination of the Nine-Patch and Log Cabin structures. The quilt was an album of memories for its maker, who associated the pieces with the persons who had worn the clothing, and it will undoubtedly be a treasured heirloom in her family, perhaps like those others, finding its way in due time into a museum collection.

The subtle effects that can be achieved by color harmony and the further challenge of arranging light and dark shades effectively have undoubtedly contributed to the popularity of Log Cabin quilts in Kentucky as elsewhere. Since the mid-nineteenth century when Mrs. Backus and later Mrs. J. A. Tichenor (Fig. 12), and others were making Log Cabin quilts now in the Kentucky Museum, the variations called Sunshine and Shade and Light and Dark Paths have intrigued Kentucky quilt-makers. For some these names include what are elsewhere called Straight Furrow, Barn Raising, and other names. The Orlofskys, in *Quilts in America* (especially pp. 310–14), discuss and illustrate the widespread popularity of these and other Log Cabin patterns.

Triangles alone can create a tantalizing sequence of

Figure 12. Section of Sunshine and Shade arrangement of Log Cabin. Mrs. J. A. Tichenor, about 1900. Kentucky Museum.

optical illusions, as in a quilt called Tents of Armageddon in Miriam Tuska's collection. "One of my all-time favorites," the owner says of this well-worn quilt, which she rescued from use as a rag on a garage floor. Alternating blue and white half-squares form the entire quilt top, constantly forming new angular patterns as the eye moves over them. A more colorful effect was achieved recently by a Warren County quilter in an arrangement of equilateral triangles that she calls Thousand Pyramids. This one also creates the illusion of constant movement and change.

Among the quilters' favorites using triangles are diversified abstractions of baskets and of pine trees, abundantly present in collections of nineteenth-century quilts and among those fresh from twentieth-century quilters' frames. Pieced basket designs, as well as certain applique patterns, were often elaborately quilted as gifts for brides. By no means are all Basket quilts constructed of triangles, however. The Basket Name Quilt in the Miriam Tuska

Figure 13. Section of Tree of Paradise (sometimes called Pine Tree). Made by Mrs. Bennett (Martha Jane) Clark, Riverside, contemporary. Mrs. Azro (Annie) Clark assisted with both piecing and quilting.

collection (Fig. 31), for example, uses triangles, squares, rectangles, and other geometric shapes.

Mrs. Sidney Chapman of Butler County and Mrs. Bradley (Winnie) James of Muhlenberg County both made quilts in Basket and Pine Tree patterns in the 1960s as good utility quilts. Martha Jane Clark saw a Pine Tree quilt when she was a girl and liked it but did not make it until she was a grandmother. Assisted by her mother-in-law, Annie Clark, she made two quilts, using green for the trees, and gave them to two of her granddaughters (Fig. 13). She calls the pattern Tree of Paradise.

Another triangle pattern found wherever old quilts are kept or new ones are made is Ocean Waves, a pattern that eighty-eight-year-old Joe Ed Chelf of Hart County makes in 1976 on the machine (Fig. 2) and Mrs. R. C. Goode of Glasgow has preserved as an heirloom from the nineteenth century. Ocean Waves is a block pattern constructed in triangles (or half-squares) in two sizes. Two large ones fill out opposite corners. In between, four rows of smaller half-squares in alternating colors run diagonally from corner to corner. When the blocks are assembled the design that emerges is a cross-hatch pattern over the entire quilt, similar to Irish Chain.

Wild Goose Chase, again constructed entirely of triangles, has appeared in Kentucky most often as a border or as a motif to separate the blocks of another pattern, such as applique Princess Feather or Fern Leaf (Fig. 26), both seen in Kentucky Museum quilts. The pattern is built on equilateral triangles placed with the tip of one touching the base of the next to form rows, often with small stars in the corners or where strips intersect to form the blocks.

Patterns with such intriguing names as Flying Geese and Birds in Air, along with stylized tulips and lilies, are other favorites based on triangles. These patterns, however far they may be from representational, suggest the movement of these things in nature. The Kaleidoscope as Mae Young made it and as Jonathan Holstein pictures it (*The Pieced Quilt*, p. 65) is an arrangement of colorful triangles that "won't stay still" as one looks at it.

The Kentucky Museum collection as well as many small private collections known to the author reveal an earlier enthusiasm for working tiny sawtooth or slim sunburst triangles into feathered or spangled patterns of stars or circles. These were much in evidence at an exhibit of quilts and coverlets by the Franklin-Simpson Chapter of the Daughters of the American Revolution at their May meeting in 1974. At that exhibit Frances and Mary Ellen Richards showed Feathered Star, Indian Summer (or Whig's Defeat), and others of this type, all exquisitely designed and crafted. One resembled the pattern the Orlofskys call New York Beauty (*Quilts in America*, p. 80). Further evidence of the popularity of these patterns appears in the equally beautiful but very different variations in the collections of Miriam Tuska of Lexington and Mrs. Jack Richardson of Glasgow (Figs. 14

and 15). These quilts have been remarkably well preserved.

A pattern of particularly interesting color and design making use of this kind of embellishment in the Kentucky Museum collection (Plate 3) is the Star of Chamblie, which is developed in the traditional colors of red, orange, pink, green, and white, and which resembles Fish Tail and Pine Cone. It is one of five quilts made by Ruth Bennett Lindley for her heirs. The initials LEL on the back of this quilt are those of the donor, Lenora E. Lindley.

A quilter asked at different times about her favorite pattern sometimes gives different answers, the reason being that she likes a number of them about equally. Always in the running are star quilts, especially the large, full-quilt-size Star of Bethlehem or Lone Star. These are based on the diamond, some being constructed entirely of this one pattern shape. Small diamonds combine to make large diamonds, which in turn form the points of the star. Kentucky quilters have made Lone Stars in cotton and silk, from cradle size to king size, in almost every imaginable combination of colors, the runaway favorite being an explosion of color that contains the entire spectrum in printed cottons. Mae Young set hers against a blue background suggestive of the sky. Always recognizable, the Lone Star quilts are seldom identical.

Chloe Meador of north Warren County placed sections of other stars in the border of her Lone Star top, enhancing the effect of the large central star by suggesting its place in a constellation. This was her favorite of the many patterns she made during her long life. Making quilts was her pleasurable activity when she could take time on wintry days between the busy season of tobacco stripping in the barn and spring planting. Unable to let her hands lie idle, she made as many as thirty quilts some winters, but not all in this pattern! Her use of brown domestic even for her best quilts, as background for the top as well as for linings, reflects her constant awareness

Figure 14 *(above)* Detail of Feathered Variable Star, maker unknown. Owned by Mrs. Jack Richardson of Glasgow, whose husband bought it at a Kentucky auction. Figure 15 *(below)* Detail of a finely crafted quilt elsewhere identified as Whig's Defeat or Indian Summer, maker unknown. Also owned by Mrs. Jack Richardson, Glasgow.

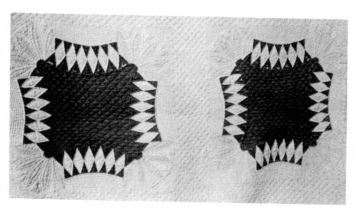

of durability. Both her Lone Star and her daughter's favorite, Broken Star, were often given as wedding gifts in the family and neighborhood, but even for these quilts her frugality in saving scraps and her emphasis on making them functional were inevitable considerations. Yet Chloe Meador was much admired as a generous person and a master craftsman among those who knew her. As so many Kentucky quilters can say, her quilts went "all over the United States," as strangers saw them and placed their orders through mutual acquaintances. She had more than a little of the artist about her as she arranged her heaps of small diamonds into that sunburst of color that delights everyone who owns a Chloe Meador Star quilt.

Mrs. Edwin Ward of Princeton was inspired by patriotic sentiment and affection for Western Kentucky University to make a red, white, and blue Lone Star quilt for the Kentucky Museum in 1975 (Plate 1). This is her Bicentennial Quilt, made entirely by hand during her seventy-second year. The nation's Bicentennial stimulated similar efforts in other parts of the state. Some are keyed more closely to history, some more closely to affairs of the Commonwealth, and most of them are more intricate. Yet the very simplicity of Mrs. Ward's quilt is appealing.

A pattern Mrs. Chelf calls Heavenly Star (Fig. 16) is one of many adaptations of the Star of LeMoyne, upon which so many star and floral patterns appear to be based, including tulips, lilies, and peonies. This pattern has sometimes been called Yankee Pride in other regions. The Kentucky Museum has an unnamed quilt in this pattern made by Edith Neighbors of Butler County in recent years. Mrs. Tuska has an older one that she calls Snow Crystals. Some modern Kentucky quilters who learn patterns from workshops and quilting manuals know the LeMoyne Star, but the dozens of names for star patterns in the Western Kentucky University Folklore and Folklife Collection do not include it. A particular type of eight-pointed star in which the points are divided

Figure 16. One block of Heavenly Star, elsewhere called Snow Crystals or Yankee Pride. Annie Chelf, contemporary.

lengthwise into contrasting triangles or in which the eight diamonds that form the points alternate in color or tone, it includes the basic motif of the Kentucky Graveyard quilt (Fig. 33) and the Heavenly Star. The name LeMoyne Star is sometimes applied more generally to eight-pointed star designs.

Kentucky quilters have won many prizes—in world's fairs, commercial textile firm contests, and periodical competitions—far too many to cite here. A recent winner of a quilt block contest sponsored by *Progressive Farmer* was Mrs. Gertrude Mitchell of Russell Springs for a pattern she called National Star, an eight-point star embellished with stitching to give an effect of radiance.

Mrs. Youree Howell of Plum Springs in Warren County likes quilts both old and new and enjoys making them.

Among her large repertory and personal store of quilts, two outstanding examples are a large star block quilt that she herself made in bright colors set against a white background, and one made in the very old Blazing Star pattern (one star superimposed on another) dated 1870 and signed by Rachel Willis, the owner's great aunt. Of another century-old quilt made by Nancy J. Willis, the owner says, "It's just a little diamond quilt," but most viewers see in it a six-point star. Both quilts have dull backgrounds and linings, but the red dyes in the stars are rich and bright.

An ingenious and charming small quilt in the Kentucky Museum in the Star and Cross pattern uses Tumbling Blocks (outside of Kentucky more often called Baby Blocks) to embellish a large cross in light colors against a background of a four-pointed star in dark shades (Plate 8). Each Tumbling Block is made of three diamonds in contrasting colors to give the effect of a cube. This three-dimensional illusion is enhanced through the use of elongated hexagons in the darker shades to set the blocks together in the cross pattern. A pleasing medium blue in the background of the top and a similar shade of basket-weave material for the lining were happy choices for contrast with the pattern. This nineteenth-century quilt, in the manner of some late twentieth-century popular art, projects other images as one continues to look at it. Diamonds make patterns other than stars, and other patches make stars, but to the average Kentucky quilt-maker, the two are virtually inseparable.

"They are everywhere in Kentucky!" exclaimed a student who had been studying Kentucky quilts, referring to the colorful Flower Garden (Grandmother's Flower Garden). "They look so hard to make," she continued, "I wonder why all of them make it." A quilter will say that only the first one is difficult, since it is made entirely of hexagons. It is necessary only to cut and sew the pieces evenly so that they will not pucker, and to assemble the blocks in a pleasing array of color. For this type of quilt

Figure 17. Flower Garden (elsewhere called Grandmother's Flower Garden). Lucille Hodges, Alvaton, contemporary.

the more ambitious workers "lay out" the pattern as to size and color harmony before cutting the pieces. Then they have only to follow their own plan to achieve the desired effect. Some quilters vary the Flower Garden, as Lucille Hodges of Alvaton did (Fig. 17), by interspersing chain borders of small green diamonds around the hexagon-shaped blocks and around the border of the quilt. The edges can be scalloped to follow the flowerlike blocks. Mrs. Bradley James of Muhlenberg County likes to make these quilts entirely in hexagons of pastel colors. She gives careful attention to color harmony and consistently uses white backings. Others use much red and other bright colors and prefer green or other colored linings as suitable settings for the "flowers."

Similar in its colorful pattern, and perennially made somewhere in the state since the latter half of the nineteenth century has been Field of Diamonds or Diamond

Field (also called Pickle Dish, although that name applies to other patterns). The same template can be used as for Flower Garden, but the quilter adds hexagons on either side of the central circle of them to form the diamond effect of each block.

In Kentucky collections, quilts built on the hexagon patch vary almost as much in fabric and color harmonies as do the Log Cabin quilts. Mrs. Mary Katherine Bryant of Bowling Green has made Diamond Field in brightly colored double-knits. The Kentucky Museum collection includes these hexagon patterns in muted cottons, in both bright and somber silks, and in the gayest of pastels. Miriam Tuska describes one in her collection, which she calls Mosaic in Diamonds, as "exquisite, subtle, and very formal."

The student's remark as to the ubiquity of Flower Gardens in Kentucky is well based. Nearly all Kentucky quilters have made at least one of this type in some delightful color combination. Embellishment with other shapes, though common, is unnecessary for the beauty of this design. As with the Lone Star quilts, no two are alike, and they can be most pleasing to their makers as scrap quilts that evoke memories of aprons, dresses, and household furnishings, their own and those of friends and relatives, over a period of years. The author values one that is made almost entirely of pieces given her mother by her grandmother, scraps from dresses she had made and worn before her death in 1935. Like Mrs. Meador, her grandmother viewed quilts as functional, but her mother has made keepsakes for her children and grandchildren in the pattern she has always considered a show quilt—the Flower Garden. The liking for quilts based on hexagons has been demonstrably durable, among the most ancient and the most modern in bed quilt history. Honeycomb and mosaic patterns are older than Kentucky, but they are well accounted for in Kentucky quilt collections, and they are clearly a part of the contemporary quilting scene.

Pieced Quilts: Curving Patterns

Patterns in the families of Four-Patch, Nine-Patch, Lone Star, and Flower Garden share the trait of using straight-sided geometric pieces to form blocks: squares, half-squares, rectangles, diamonds, and hexagons. Another cluster of patterns shares combinations of these forms with curves of various kinds ranging from circles to serpentine meanders.

A remarkable cluster of patterns develops from a simple cutout which can be arranged in such different ways that the neophyte can hardly believe only two pattern shapes are involved. The two are made by drawing an arc across the corner of a square of cloth to yield a quarter-circle for one, the remainder of the square for the other. Such patches in two colors can then be manipulated into patterns as different as Drunkard's Path, with its zig-zagging lines across the quilt, and the swastika-like Wonder of the World or I Wish You Well (Fig. 48). Marguerite Ickis in *The Standard Book of Quilt Making and Collecting* (pp. 74–77) demonstrates a dozen others without exhausting the possibilities. As with the single pattern shape, color variations extend the range.

Kentucky quilters who consider their work strictly of the everyday variety rarely undertake to work with this family of patterns, since piecing circles and arcs is more tedious than straight-edged pieces for the average quiltmaker. Quilters like Ellen Barrow and Annie Chelf love them because they offer a stimulating challenge to be creative. Rose Brite of Warren County must have liked these patterns. Among the many quilts she bequeathed to her nieces and great-nieces are Balloon, Robbing Peter to Pay Paul, and Drunkard's Path, which some prefer to call Rocky Road to Dublin. Mrs. Pauline Lehr of Riverside exhibited at a quilters' workshop in December 1975 a Drunkard's Path that had been in her husband's family since it was rescued from the great Chicago fire, four generations ago (Fig. 18).

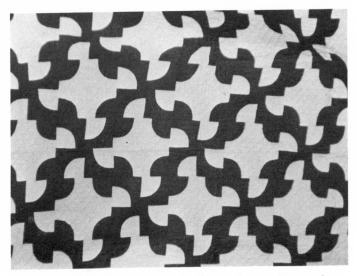

Figure 18. Drunkard's Path (Trail), displayed at a quilting workshop by Pauline Lehr in 1975. Late nineteenth century.

Probably the most commonly recognized pattern, and one that has rivaled even the Lone Star and Flower Garden as suitable for Bride's Quilts and other best quilts, is based on curving shapes—the Double Wedding Ring, more commonly called in Kentucky simply Wedding Ring. Typically, the block is constructed of a small square, a large ellipse, and the tiny sections of an arc that make the large overlapping circles of the ring. Like those other favorites, Flower Garden and Postage Stamp, the Wedding Ring uses assorted small scraps and emerges with the charm of many colors. Joining four blocks with the large ellipse patterns in a petallike arrangement produces in the overall view large overlapping circles, with small Four-Patches at the intersections. Some very precise needlewomen maintain the curving lines even at the intersections, still approximating the Four-Patch pattern there.

This pattern, according to Patsy and Myron Orlofsky

Figure 19. Small section of Double Wedding Ring. Note quilted lyres. Flossie Sheriff McClure, Lexington, early twentieth century. Miriam Tuska collection.

(*Quilts in America*, p. 230), was popular as a Bride's Quilt from the late nineteenth century. It was well established in the Kentucky area as a best quilt by the 1930s. The Miriam Tuska collection contains one made by Flossie Sheriff McClure (Fig. 19) with stuffed lyres in the white areas, craftsmanship comparable to that of the early nineteenth-century white quilt featuring trapunto. The cotton stuffing was so firm in the McClure quilt that it has worn through to the surface here and there during the half century or more since its creation. Many quilters consistently use a background of white and white lining for their Wedding Rings, but others use a bright color. Ellen Barrow used sunshine yellow for one. Lavender and blue frequently form the background.

Akin to the Wedding Ring in its use of tiny scraps forming arcs is Snake Trail (Plate 4), which may well have been influenced by the older woven coverlet design bearing the name Snail Trail. Snake Trail is set together with arcs of white or contrasting color to form square blocks. Assembly of the blocks forms the sinuous trails across the quilt. Winnie James of Penrod kept the templates for Snake Trail always at hand as her choice of a pattern to use up small scraps. When she accumulated enough pieces for a top, she pieced it and soon after quilted it in the same characteristic sinuous trails. She has made many in this pattern in her lifetime.

More popular than Snake Trail has been the Fan quilt in all its variations, many of which are pieced in arcs to form quarter circles. Some quilters have several Fans in their repertories. Bonnie Willis and Hattie Howell both have made these from different templates and in different arrangements, some with the pattern in the block, some with the fans set in straight-across or diagonal rows. Some Basket patterns, such as Rose Brite's, are constructed of pattern pieces similar to those of the Fans. Reminiscent of an era when they were essential for comfort and significant as ornaments, like baskets and other useful items of earlier domestic life, fans survive on quilts because of their pleasing form.

Complex Pieced Patterns

If the preceding discussion of some of the opportunities for individualized basic patterns has suggested a wide range of added complexities, one need only look at a few of the combinations of these to understand the rationale for the title of this chapter—their infinite variety. The two pattern pieces which produce Drunkard's Path, for instance, can become more complex by one additional step. An elaboration of removing a quarter circle from one corner of a square of cloth is to remove another quarter circle from the opposite corner of the square. The pieces can then be assembled to produce a novel block called Devil's Backbone by Kitty Kurath of Monroe County and Bertha Anderson of Livingston County.

Gertrude Blair of Eli, in Russell County, won first prize in a 1944 quilt block contest sponsored by the *Kentucky Farm Home Journal* for her fifteen-inch block, Star and Crescent. This pattern, also called Star of the Four Winds, can be pieced and then appliqued to the block. Here the four diamonds that form the star alternate with slim crescent-rimmed sectors resembling longitudinal sections of an ice cream cone. Miss Blair believed the pattern to be a variant of an early Pennsylvania Dutch design. The visual pleasure provided by its changing optical effects is characteristic of many of those earlier patterns.

The option of using strips to frame a block, or of using a running pattern such as Wild Goose Chase (as in Fig. 26) or the chained squares of a Simple Irish Chain to separate pattern blocks adds another dimension to pattern variability. Such variations occur in appliqued as well as pieced quilts.

A pattern elevating the familiar Nine-Patch to eye-teasing complexity is variously known as Young Man's Fancy and Goose in the Pond (Fig. 20). Here the individual pieces of a framed Nine-Patch are subdivided: four small Nine-Patch pieces for the four corners, the four remaining pieces made up of three parallel bars each, and the center piece left undivided. This pattern on Lelia Price's Album top adds a small center star and is designed in red, white, and blue.

Another interesting pieced quilt in the Kentucky Museum is a large sunburst pattern designated Sunflower, a name that applies to many variations in both pieced and appliqued quilts. This one, made about the middle of the nineteenth century by Amanda Mitchell and bequeathed to her granddaughter Pearl Holman of Bowling Green, equals the Lindley Star of Chamblie quilt in its intricacies of color patterning and its skillful use of extremely small pieces. Nine large sunburst blocks are spaced out with quilted stars and tulips in the white areas such as commonly appeared in Bride's Quilts of the period.

Figure 20. One block of Young Man's Fancy or Goose-in-the-Pond. Made for Stephen Enscore by a member of his family, mid-nineteenth century. Kentucky Museum.

Although very few Kentucky quilters of the 1970s work with such intricate and time-consuming pieced designs as these, the impulse that prompted them still lives. The fascination of forming patterns with minute bits of color is part of Flora Free's guiding principle as she varies both arrangement and color schemes in a pattern she calls Pepper and Salt Shakers (Fig. 21). The pattern originally combined seven small variegated hexagons (each one pieced from small triangles around the central hexagon) into a large snowflake-like design set together with contrasting solid color, creating an illusion of spokes radiating from the central hexagon to the six corners of the larger hexagon. This pattern is sometimes called Seven Sisters. Mrs. Free decided to "try out" small hexagon blocks set against a solid or white background, and liked the effect so well that she made a group of very special quilts in the design. For each of her sons who had served in one or more of America's wars she pieced a Pepper and

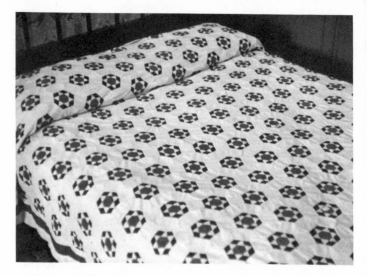

Figure 21 *(above)* Pepper and Salt Shakers in red, white, and blue. Unquilted top used as a coverlet. Flora Free, Penrod, contemporary. Figure 22 *(below)* Flora Free, assisted by author Mary Clarke, brings her Dove in the Window out on the porch. The predominant color is orange.

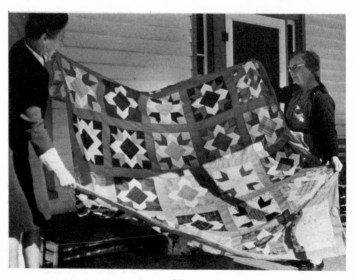

Salt Shakers quilt in patriotic colors—red, white, and blue. In memory of her deceased husband, who served during World War I, she pieced one of these and added a border so that she could use it on a bed in her own home as an unquilted coverlet. To her the quilts commemorate the patriotic sentiment that motivated the soldiers in her family and the happy relief their survival afforded when the anxious war years were over. Mrs. Free has other patterns for other occasions, such as Dove in the Window for family weddings, an intricate pattern involving at least three colors (Fig. 22). A modification of an eight-point star, it can be viewed as four flying doves with beaks toward the center.

Appliqued Quilts

Although it is convenient to segregate pieced work from applique as different kinds of patchwork, the two activities are not always separate. Applique generally refers to designs cut out and sewed onto a quilt-size continuous backing. Some of the designs sewed onto the backing are pieced beforehand, however, so that an appliqued Dresden Plate, for example, is also piecework. Some appliqued quilts are also made in blocks, the applique designs being fixed to separate blocks for subsequent assembly.

Since applique can be more pictorial than piecework, the sky is the limit for design possibilities. Yet only a few basic groups of motifs have accounted for the great majority of applique patterns: floral and leaf designs, stylized human and animal figures, and household objects. Kentucky quilters interviewed for this discussion unanimously considered applique tops more time-consuming, and a majority considered applique quilts more beautiful and valuable than pieced ones. Many of them combined piecing, applique, and embroidery on their favorites in this category. Annie Chelf's most valued production is her Oriental Poppy applique quilt (Plate 5). Another prized possession is a pieced and appliqued Tulip Basket family heirloom quilt. Bonnie Willis considered her Ohio Rose superior to even her beautiful Star, Fan, and Wedding Ring quilts. Evidently a thief who broke into her house one day in 1974 agreed. The Ohio Rose, in use as a guest bed coverlet, disappeared—nothing else!

Tulips and lilies (both designations are applied to the same patterns) reflect the taste of the quilters. They vary from the elegant simplicity of small floral motifs against elaborately quilted white backgrounds to splashy designs with gay bands of color separating the blocks. Ellen Barrow's version is of the pieced and appliqued variety with four blossoms joined in the center in a cross-shaped meeting of stems. Mrs. Bradley James's pieced and appliqued tulip is angular, hinting at cubist style, set at an angle in the block. A quilt in the Franklin D. A. R. exhibit (Fig. 23) shows three blossoms stylized on a single stem, a mere accent of red and green against a great expanse of exquisite quilting. No name is attached but it is of the type sometimes called Virginia Lily or North Carolina Lily. The Miriam Tuska collection contains a quilt of similar quality and somewhat more faded elegance in a pattern rare in Kentucky, the Lotus. Sadie's Choice (Rose) in Mrs. Chelf's repertory is akin to these older floral designs, and the quality of Chelf quilting is quite artistic "modern." The roses, sunflowers, lilies, and tulips, though numerous in their quilt variations, are suggestive rather than representative of the range of floral applique quilts in the state, and they overlap at times with leaf patterns.

Mrs. Elbert (Noka) Beck of north Warren County decided in 1975 to finish a pieced and appliqued Sunflower top begun by her husband's aunt, Mattie Cole, who died in 1918 leaving it incomplete. Mrs. Beck padded and embroidered the large brown centers of the sunflowers and quilted it by the piece (Fig. 24). Mrs. Cora Lee Keen of Butler County made her Sunflower and Tulip applique designs more representational, leaving no doubt as to

Figure 23 *(above)* Section of Tulip appliqued quilt, maker and date unknown. Displayed at a D.A.R. exhibit, Franklin, 1974. Figure 24 *(below)* One block of Sunflower. Pieced and appliqued by Mattie Cole before 1918, embroidered and quilted by Noka Beck, Hadley, 1975.

Figure 25. One block of Nebraska Red Leaf. This unquilted top was made as a wedding gift by Cora Kincaid Bragg in her eighty-fifth year.

what flower was depicted. Some quilters place the flowers in baskets or pots.

Since the tulip poplar with its tulip-shaped leaf was long considered Kentucky's state tree, and since its simple shape lends itself easily to both pieced and appliqued representation, it appears in many collections (Plate 3). Somewhat more complicated oak, maple, palm, and other leaf patterns appear with less frequency, usually offering a recognizable approximation of the real thing. The names and details of floral and leaf patterns can be adapted to the quilter's taste or whim. An example of extending such a pattern considerably beyond the pictorial into an attractive block design is one called Nebraska Red Leaf (Fig. 25), which is, despite the name, reported to have originated in Kentucky. (Such things are difficult to trace and harder to prove.) The maker pieced the top while in her eighties as a wedding gift.

The family of nineteenth-century patterns approximating the swastika, or a wheel of plumes, includes

Figure 26. Section of Fern Leaf or Princess Feather, with a Wild Goose Chase border. Jane Jinsey Gray, about 1850. Kentucky Museum.

appliqued as well as pieced patterns. Fern Leaf and Princess Feather appear on the records of the Kentucky Museum. Jane Jinsey Gray of Dimple Community in Butler County, whose life very nearly spanned the nineteenth century, is reported to have spun and woven the cloth for a museum quilt in Fern Leaf (Fig. 26). It is now fragile and ragged but still exhibits beautiful craftsmanship. As in several other museum quilts of this period, the applique pattern is in a dainty dark blue print against a white background. Another in a closely similar pattern appears to be of the same dark blue material as old bandannas. The maker, Martha Stockton Mitchell, who died in 1843, is said to have been a niece of Richard Stockton, one of the signers of the Declaration of Independence. This quilt also is somewhat ragged but shows the touch of a highly skilled quilter. A star appears at the center where the leaves or plumes join.

Contemporary quilters who are still attracted to these patterns that convey some illusion of movement are more likely to use feathers and plumes in the quilting than in the applique pattern. Quilt kits somewhat simplify the difficulty of cutting and putting together some patterns for those who do not feel the compulsion to make their own from start to finish. But the quilting is rarely as fine as in the early quilts, Flossie Sheriff McClure's work being a notable exception. In the past, as now, it is possible that some quilts were made from commercial patterns or even from kits. Yet little details of quilting or embellishment of details makes each of these quilts a unique expression of the quilter's taste and imagination.

Dogs, cats, horses, birds, and other motifs from the animal world appear in scattered places. A Horse quilt in the Eubank family of Simpson County is quite pictorial and has embroidered on it the names of horses whose representations appear in profile—Dandelion, Betsy Rose, and Rocket. Jewell Eubank, present owner of the quilt and longtime riding instructor, commented that the horses portrayed on the quilt were real horses that had been family favorites. In Simpson County, where horses are prized and where the annual Mule Day is an important festival, both types of animals can inspire enough affection to be commemorated in this way. An occasional quilter will make her own pattern to represent a dog she likes or has owned, as Bertha Rice of Johnson County did, but the Scottie pattern used to make children's quilts has probably outdistanced all other dog motifs. Mrs. Joe (Bonnie) Willis of Riverside made every dog of a different print, appliqued each diagonally onto a small white square, and alternated the dog squares with contrasting squares of pin-checked gingham (Fig. 27).

Popular as domestic and farm animals may be, none of them can approach the butterfly as a pattern inspiration. As with roses, sunflowers, and tulips, the variations in Butterfly quilts are notable and colorful. Kentucky quilter Pearl McDyer of Campbell County contributed to *Kentucky Farmer* an attractive butterfly pattern that used arcs of print scraps in the spread wings, in the manner of Snake Trail and Wedding Ring piecing. A Disney-like fantasy sometimes appears, but close pictorial resem-

Figure 27. Section of a Scottie Dog quilt. Appliqued, embroidered, and quilted by Mrs. Joe Willis, Riverside, contemporary.

blance to real butterflies is even more popular. Here and there a cubist effect produces a blocky, substantial type not seen in nature. The quilter's imagination can run riot on butterflies, and the diversity of these quilts suggests that few have felt bound by a pattern. Cora Lee Keen of Sugar Grove Community in Butler County made a gay Butterfly applique quilt and stripped the blocks together with narrow bars of bright color (Fig. 28). During her husband's years of invalidism in the late 1960s and early 1970s, she made quilts so that she could keep him company and yet feel that she was doing something useful.

The House quilt is pieced but is so pictorial that it seems more at home with the applique quilts. Both pattern and name vary but basic structure for this novelty quilt still holds—a small house with a roof, one or two chimneys, a door, and windows. Dessie Embry of Morgantown, leader of the quilters who meet in the Morgantown Public Library each week, likes to make every house of a different color (Fig. 29), producing a quilt as brightly colored as Joseph's coat (incidentally another Kentucky quilt name). A few have been made entirely in red and black as the Little Red Schoolhouse. A Ruby McKim pattern (*One Hundred and One Patchwork Patterns*, p. 117) called it House on the Hill and referred to it (in 1931) as an old-time pattern. The basic pattern appears to be from the nineteenth century. Jonathan Holstein

Figure 28. Section of a Butterfly quilt. Pieced, appliqued, embroidered, and quilted by Cora Lee Keen, Butler County, contemporary.

Figure 29. Section of a House quilt, with each house in a different fabric. A good example of representational piecework. Dessie Embry, Morgantown, contemporary.

pictures a New Hampshire variant of about 1880 and writes, "The objects are reduced to their basic forms and extraneous decoration is removed; the same general process occurred, say, in the conversion of a bottle into the form it took on a Cubist canvas. The object retains its general characteristics, in abstracted form" [*The Pieced Quilt*, p. 119, Plate 62]. The McKim pattern calls for seven pattern shapes, not difficult to cut or assemble. Blocks may or may not be separated by contrasting strips, and quilting follows the pattern "by the piece."

By far the most popular representation of a human figure in applique for at least fifty years has been the Dutch Doll, which seems to have a close affiliation with Sunbonnet Girl (or Baby) and other simplified abstractions of bonneted little girls. Among the rich legacy of quilts left by Rose Brite of Warren County, a beloved unmarried aunt who has surviving namesakes in three later generations, are quilts made in this pattern for children of the family. In 1975 one of these was in use in the home of Mrs. Hobson (June Rose) Sinclair in Bowling

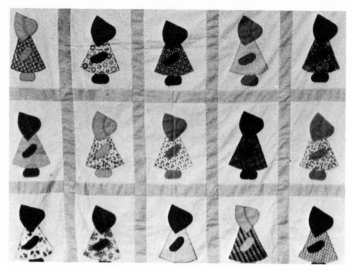

Figure 30. Dutch Doll (also called Little Dutch Girl). Mrs. Joe Willis, Riverside, contemporary.

Green, while another was in New York in the home of her daughter Elizabeth Rose, and a third was in the Bowling Green apartment of Mrs. Sinclair's mother, Rose Swaim. These quilts are in pastel shades against a white background. Bonnie Willis made hers in bright and varied prints (Fig. 30). Although this pattern appears less often in quilting manuals than do some related patterns, it persists as a perennial favorite among the quilters interviewed for this discussion. It is often made of scraps from the clothing of the child who is to receive the gift quilt.

Mrs. Bertha Rice liked the Little Dutch Girl and made it by a pattern she received from a neighbor, but she adapted it to her own fancy. "The pattern didn't show anything at all in the little girl's hands. And I thought she needed something, so I embroidered this little flower in her hand," pointing to the quilt on the bed. "I tried to make a different flower in each little girl's hand on the quilt. I imagined 'em out in a field agatherin' flowers." Popular as the Dutch Girl (Boy, Dollie) may be, with many patterns available, six different quilters are likely to produce six quite different conceptions as to color and arrangement.

Novelty and Special Occasion Quilts

Along with the charm of the familiar has come the charm of novelty. Some Kentucky quilters have made Yo-Yo quilts, stenciled pictorial quilts, cross-stitched and other embroidered quilts, and others assembled by folding and tacking squares. Somewhere in a quilting family of more than one generation is likely to be a Yo-Yo or Bon-Bon quilt or sofa pillow, described by the Orlofskys as "shirred rosettes whipped together at the edges" [p. 225]. These happy impractical creations were made of calicos, other cottons, or silks. Shirley Leath of Alvaton has a Yo-Yo pillow made early in this century by her great-grandmother, Mrs. George Washington (Nancy) Lawrence of Adairville. Nancy Lawrence's Wedding Ring was used, incidentally, in contemporary Kentucky artist Don Ensor's print "Stitching Time." Mrs. Lawrence appears to have enjoyed work many quilters would consider tedious. "She was very precise in her work," says Shirley Leath, who treasures even more than her Yo-Yo pillow a Flower Garden quilt by the same maker. "She used a pattern for every piece." Mrs. Leath, who uses her great-grandmother's frame and credits Mrs. Lawrence with inspiring her to take pride in quilting, quilted a cross-stitch top made by another member of her family, but she prefers and makes pieced quilts.

Not only cross-stitch, but other types of embroidery have intrigued quilters of the 1970s. Stenciled designs, sometimes requiring textile paints and simple embroidery stitches as well as quilting stitches for their completion, have been available in kits. Several of these are discussed elsewhere in this book—history quilts, scripture quilts, state flower quilts, and the like. Some of these are, of course, original creations of their makers, or have personal or local embellishments, such as Flossie Good-dall's states quilt.

In the present decade the novelty quilt all admire but many consider too tedious to make is Cathedral Windows, which is not quilted at all. This design, made by energetic quilt-makers like Hattie Howell of Plum Springs and Mary Wallace of Glasgow Road in Barren County, involves a technique of folding and tacking layers of cloth in contrasting colors, usually with un-bleached muslin or some other white material as the outside layer, so that the colors show through the "window" created by folding (Plate 4). A variation on this, achieving a similar effect by similar techniques, is used by Mabel Howard of Smith's Grove, who calls it Jacob's Windows.

Some special-occasion quilts achieve novelty by their function rather than their structure or pattern. All over Kentucky are proud owners of Friendship Quilts or Presentation Quilts that bring to mind family, neighbors, friends, or special events in their lives. Maxine Gilley of Metcalfe County received hers as a wedding gift. Blanche Critser's was a 1938 gift from her Sunday school class at the Petersburg Church and was made in Friendship Ring pattern. Charles Guthrie treasures one given him in his native Cumberland County in the 1930s. Each person contributing to it pieced a block in a pattern resembling Courthouse Square, with the name of the giver and some-times the date embroidered in the center. The Miriam Tuska collection contains a Friendship Quilt in a Basket pattern with a name written in indelible ink inside the handle of each basket (Fig. 31). Mrs. Doc Miller of Rock Bridge has a particularly interesting one made before her lifetime. "At that time different people would piece a square and put whatever decoration they wanted to on it and give it to the quilter." In one square of the quilt the donor had written, "Hope Little Frank's Tottering Around Me Today, May 27 96."

Presentation Quilts, which overlap Friendship Quilts,

Figure 31. Detail of a pieced Basket quilt with names written below the handles. Miriam Tuska collection.

continue to be given to ministers by church members (women usually make blocks for the men in their families as well as for themselves) and sometimes to a loved teacher or friend. Not all Name Quilts are Friendship Quilts, nor do all Friendship and Presentation Quilts bear names, but they do often overlap. The practice of giving them has persisted for more than a century.

Little evidence has come to the author's attention that Kentucky quilters have made Album Quilts, common in other regions. (In the Baltimore area, for example, they appear to have been made as Bride's Quilts, Memory Quilts, and simply to record a quilter's repertory of patterns.) Lelia Price of the Hadley Community in Warren County found an Album Quilt top in her attic after her husband's death but she has no idea who made it, why, or when (Plate 1). Since the house had been her husband's family's home, she associated the mystery top with one of his aunts.

Memorial Quilts may have been more numerous in Kentucky at some earlier time than present family and museum holdings reflect. Notable, of course, is the Kentucky Graveyard quilt (Figs. 33, 34), discussed in a later chapter. A number of Memorial Quilts, some of them parlor throws, are known to be in private hands, but some other types, such as the black and white Widow's Quilt and Eli Lilly Death Watch Quilt (Album type), if they exist or ever did in Kentucky, are unknown to this author.

Historical subjects and patriotic sentiment have inspired far too many Kentucky quilts to enumerate here. Mrs. Carl Clark of Glasgow has a History Quilt picturing major events and figures. Mrs. Walter (Pauline) Lehr of Riverside has an unquilted History top pieced and embroidered in red, white, and blue by Mary Ann Calhoun, her husband's grandmother, about 1914. A number of centennial and bicentennial quilts commemorate those landmark years.

The foregoing has been a sampling of quilt patterns found in Kentucky, with emphasis on those in the south-central region of the state. Where did the quilters find their patterns? In the day when quilting bees were more common, the best source was personal exchange. June Sinclair recalls going along with her Aunt Rose and her grandmother to family bees. Patterns were exchanged as freely as news and gossip among this older generation of cousins. The Good Neighbors still exchange patterns.

Boxes of old patterns clipped from *Comfort, Kentucky Farmer, Kentucky Farm Home Journal, Modern Woodman,* and other periodicals, including newspaper features, suggest another source. Ada Guthrie Bryson and Mae Young are only two of many who have saved clippings for many years. Pauline Lehr was carrying a handful of pamphlets ordered from *McCall's* at a 1975 quilting workshop. Even Mae Young mentions buying patterns from Mountain Mist and other manufacturers of quilt batting, who sometimes issue patterns on the wrappers and invite orders for precut kits. Annie Chelf is not alone in taking patterns from older quilts or pictures of them. She also states that she has dreamed quilt patterns and then executed them. One instance was her dream of a little tulip applique which she described in enough detail for her daughter to make the quilt. It won first prize at the World's Fair exhibit in 1948.

Less common sources reported are a design from a buggy harness, a friend's wallpaper, a linoleum pattern on a neighbor's floor, and a crossword puzzle. Flora Free once took an idea from a Ritz Cracker box—a flowerlike design of pieced-together circles around a barred center circle that produced a refreshingly simple and attractive quilt block, the entire top looking like a stylized field of flowers. Mary Hope Wright of Hardin County, who was a member of the Women's Army Corps during World War II, likes to create her own patterns. "It gives me a chance to use my mind by making up my own designs," she says, speaking for other creative quilters across the state.

The materials and techniques of quilting permit much experimentation, whether the quilter works in geometric or applique patchwork designs or with varied methods of embroidering, tacking, painting, and quilting to produce strikingly different overall effects. The nature of the medium, however, requires a high degree of abstraction and ingenuity on the part of those who create masterpieces, whether the quilt be pieced, appliqued, or developed in some novelty technique.

If Kentucky quilters have produced few unique masterpieces, the evidence overwhelmingly reveals their significant role in contributing beauty along with comfort as they have worked within a craft tradition that has historical depth as well as geographical spread. Many of them have echoed the sentiment expressed by the title character in Eliza Calvert Hall's *Aunt Jane of Kentucky*: "These quilts is my album and diaries."

4

THE EXTRAVAGANT
AND EXTRAORDINARY

TRADITIONAL piecework patterns are usually produced without much reference to a particular time or place. A fancy patchwork parlor throw, in contrast, quite often reflects place, time, or theme as well as something about its creator. A commonly executed piecework quilt such as a Nine-Patch or Double Wedding Ring does, of course, reveal a great deal about the skill, patience, and color preferences of its maker, but the traditional nature of the pattern is a relatively fixed form, leaving little room for individual or topical expression. To find a quilt that is necessarily a Kentucky artifact, or one that conveys a particular Kentucky expression, the searcher has riches to choose from in the old-fashioned Crazy Quilts and similar extravagantly contrived pieces.

Here we see one-of-a-kind creations of amazing variety and complexity, quite often signed and dated by the artists, some of whom spent years on a single project of this kind. The materials, needlework, and original content suggest that some women felt a competitive urge to outdo all others in building a monument to their skill. To make a unique quilt some turned to personalities, historic events, or their environment, recording aspects of their time and place in the best medium available to them.

It would be difficult to choose the most "Kentucky" from all the examples available, but if one were to choose on the basis of Bluegrass pride in an equine tradition, local flora and fauna, and romantic legends, one could find a quilt which reflects all these and more—the Chester Dare quilt.

In the great heritage of Kentucky saddle horses a distinguished line of ancestors, including such horses as Washington Denmark, King William, Mollie, and Black Squirrel, produced a magnificent bay stallion in 1882, Chester Dare. He lived until 1904 and he was prominent in Kentucky saddle horse circles during most of that long life-span. In 1877 a young housewife in Warren County, Annie Hines Miller, started on an intricate parlor throw. Working with pieces of smooth durable woolens and heavy fine-textured cottons lavishly stitched with colored ornamental stitching that varied from one piece to another, she took several years to complete the quilt. She enriched the effect by embroidery on the patches, depicting themes of her rural life—flowers, birds, and animals. She worked her own signature into the finished product after she had appliqued a remarkable velvet portrait of Chester Dare as a centerpiece. According to family legend, hairs from Chester Dare's tail were carried by riverboat to New Orleans to use in shopping for a piece of velvet that would match the horse properly for the portrait (Plate 7).

Legend adds that Annie was much younger than her husband and that he was so jealous of her that he was overly zealous about keeping her at home. If so, he may have unwittingly contributed to the completion of her masterpiece. It is also said that he carried away her shoes when he was absent from home, that she once decided to walk barefoot to her mother's neighboring farm in the snow, and died at the age of twenty-six from the resulting pneumonia. These romantic associations combine with rare skill of execution and beauty to make the well-preserved Chester Dare quilt a prized family heirloom. It is

Figure 32. Center detail of Civil War Memorial Quilt dated 1866. Maker probably a member of the Porter family, according to donor Henry Porter Brown. Kentucky Museum.

in the possession of Annie Miller's great niece, Mrs. Nina McGinnis Stone Venable.

Just as the Chester Dare quilt captures a bit of Bluegrass history, a Memorial Quilt in the Kentucky Museum (Fig. 32) captures a bit of Kentucky Civil War history. Unfortunately for the researcher, this Memorial Quilt is worn almost to tatters and its maker is unidentified. "Found in a drawer after Mother died" is the cryptic notation that came with the donation, yet a considerable amount of information is implicit in the piece itself.

The overall pattern is a six-pointed star pieced in hexagon blocks of the Flower Garden type. The quilt is lined with silk in a small black-and-white check pattern. The total effect is rather stark. Hexagons of black velvet are among the best preserved. The other colors include dark hues of blue and red. The very fragile and worn condition of the whole piece derives largely from the insubstantial nature of fancy silks and velvets worked into the pattern. This quilt is one of those combinations of exceptional

78

needlework, decorative embroidery, and the luxurious materials associated with parlor throws, appearing in a tightly disciplined pieced top.

The central hexagon of black velvet captures immediate attention. Neatly embroidered in gold thread is "Vic W.S./A.D. 1866." The suggestion that this is a Civil War memorial is immediately verified by the constellation of names that appear in the outer rim of black hexagons of this central block. An intervening row of rich red velvet hexagons provides contrast for the gold-embroidered black hexagons. Embroidered in one of these outer pieces is "Gens. of C.S.A." Other pieces in this ring contain familiar names: Zollicoffer, Davis, Stonewall, Stewart, Buckner, Morgan. Some names are no longer legible—the delicate embroidery has worn away. But enough remains to show the maker's intention to memorialize Confederate leaders she admired, some of whom had lost their lives in the Civil War.

The six points of the large overall star show similar constellations. Each legible central piece contains a first name or nickname: Robert, Tom, Ches, Willie, and others. Around each of these is a circle of names. Around "Robert," for instance, are Dr. Stallard, Graham, Minerva, S. Huston, and others. Around "Tom" are Dr. Combs, Clara, Richard, G. Caruthers, and others. Many names are familiar. Portraits of A. Strange and M. Winans hang in the Kentucky Museum; both names appear on the quilt. There is no question about the identity of Zollicoffer. But who are Tillie, Mattie, and Betty?

Some of the familiar names suggest strongly that the unknown quilter lived in Bowling Green, not surprising since the city was for a brief time the Confederate capital of the state. Ravages of war hardened political attitudes. The 1866 date is a reminder of Lowell Harrison's closing statement in *The Civil War in Kentucky:* "It has been said with considerable truth that Kentucky joined the Confederacy after the war was over."

The Memorial Quilt casts a kind of melancholy pall

over its observer. One is tempted to speculate that "Vic W.S." was a loved one lost in the war. Did the quilter, prompted by strong emotion, set out to create the most elaborate memorial her skill could produce? Did she know the generals and other officers whose names she worked into those small hexagons? Were Tillie and Mattie fellow mourners, or just close and sympathetic friends? This tantalizing quilt surely invites further attention from a curious historian.

It is a reminder also of the kind of romantic melancholy fashionable at the time of its creation—of melodrama, mournful ballads, and obituary verse. It belongs to the same kind of artistic impulse that produced Kentucky's much-publicized Graveyard quilt (Figs. 33, 34), now in the custody of the Kentucky Historical Society. As Miriam Tuska writes of this quilt (*Kentucky Antiques*, p. 784), "Its subject matter affords us a fascinating insight into a view of death as a continuation of family involvement." The quilt was made in 1839 in the Vanceburg vicinity of Lewis County by Elizabeth Roseberry Mitchell. It is a document of social history, reflecting both the gothic romanticism that dominated much popular literature of the period and the homely domestic and religious values of ordinary people of that time and place. The basic background motif is the LeMoyne Star in sombertans and browns. But the features that make it extraordinary are the graveyard at the center with its appliqued coffins bearing the names of dead members of the family and the lined-up coffins near its entrance bearing the names of family members still living at that time. Evidently the quilt-maker's intention was that as each person died the appliqued coffin bearing his name would be moved into the cemetery. Other coffins along the border opposite the graveyard entrance may have been added at a later time. "One of the most bizarre of all the Memory quilts," the Orlofskys comment in *Quilts in America* (p. 226).

Yet another kind of Memory Quilt is found in the

unique expression of Mrs. Maggie D. Williams, whose souvenir-piece Crazy Quilt is in the collection of the Kentucky Museum. Although Mrs. Williams died young of tuberculosis and left a record of her illness in the quilt she made before she died, the sadness of her story is somehow surmounted by the indomitable spirit so clearly reflected in her own statement (Plate 7). Among those who sent her pieces to be worked into the quilt were public figures such as Jefferson Davis, president of the Confederacy; the great Kentucky journalist, Henry Watterson; and a congressman from Woodford County, J. S. G. Blackburn. The name of another artistic Kentucky quilter appears—Alice Tichenor of Ohio County. The gift pieces that accumulated between 1886 and the time of Mrs. Williams's death in 1898 also include such familiar names in the area as Kinsolving, McHenry, Beck, Morrison, Cleveland, and Cox.

This quilt illustrates dramatically the projection of the quilter's life into her creation. Near the center is a handwritten verse (Fig. 35):

> Since Aug. 1886, this quilt I have made
> Without a lesson in art to give me aid.
> And though the work may not be artistically wrought
> With pleasant memories it is fraught;
> And besides a joy, this truth I have proved,
> That distress, by industry, may be removed.

On another part of the quilt is the exhortation "Offer unto God Thanksgiving," and on another piece "Every cloud has a silver lining." Maggie Williams's gravestone in the No Creek Baptist Church cemetery near Hartford, Kentucky, is one kind of memorial to this gentle Kentucky housewife, but her brightly colored and lovingly stitched museum quilt, well preserved by her daughter, Leona Williams Hoover, and her granddaughter, Frances Hoover Loving, communicates much more of her warm friendliness and the strong character that could come to

Figure 33 *(above)* Kentucky Graveyard quilt. The basic pattern is LeMoyne Star, pieced of cotton in tans, browns, and white. Made by Elizabeth Roseberry Mitchell, Lewis County, 1839. Photograph courtesy of the Kentucky Historical Society.

Figure 34 *(right)* Center detail of Graveyard quilt showing four family coffins labelled and appliqued into previously stitched outlines of their plots. The appliqued fence and gate are decorated with embroidered green vines and pink flowers.

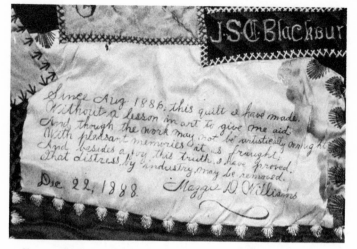

Figure 35. Center detail of Maggie Williams's Friendship Quilt.
Hartford, late nineteenth century. Kentucky Museum.

grips with suffering and early death through concentrating on happy memories of family and friends. The careful work in this artistic creation reminds even strangers almost a century later of a young woman who died well when she could no longer live well.

Some other colorful Crazy Quilts in the Kentucky Museum collection illustrate the endless possibilities for decorative motifs. The only limits appear to be those imposed by the quilter's imagination and the time available to create them. A dazzling example of variety in vivid colors appears on a quilt bearing the date 1889 and the initials A.M.L. (Fig. 36). Its maker was Anna Maria (Lively) Campbell, who lived in central Warren County. Mrs. Campbell embroidered on it representations of flowers, birds, animals, and other reminders of her environment, and inanimate objects such as a basket, a horseshoe, and a fan. The fan is pieced and then appliqued to the background piece. The central motif is red tiger lilies with stems, and the red velvet border has an embroidered

Figure 36. Section of a Crazy Quilt by Anna Maria (Lively) Campbell, 1889. Kentucky Museum.

running floral decoration. No sad story attaches to Mrs. Campbell's creation. It suggests a sunny disposition. Museum personnel reflect this quality by referring to the quilt affectionately as the Anna Quilt. The little town of Anna has disappeared from the Kentucky landscape, but the name of the quilt and its maker provide an interesting sidelight on the old place name.

Another fancy quilt in the Kentucky Museum bearing a similar range of media and motifs has the monogram W.H.G. and a machine-quilted glazed border. The quilt was made, probably in 1883–1884, by Mrs. Hubert (Trannie Buchanan) Graham for her son, Lawrence Graham of Bowling Green, who gave it to the museum. A picture of this quilt with accompanying article appeared in the Louisville *Courier-Journal* on March 6, 1949. This quilt is especially interesting for the great variety of fancy stitching. No two adjacent pieces bear the same stitching design. Some of the figures are stuffed—a technique usually associated with whitework—and some appear to be made separately or cut out of other (older?) work and appliqued. The striving for variety and novelty in this instance suggests rather strongly that the quilter was under the influence of late nineteenth-century popular periodicals which advertised materials, designs, and patterns for ornate patchwork.

Before German politics and World War II made it unpopular, the swastika was one of the ancient symbols commonly associated with good luck. One ornate quilt in the Kentucky Museum combines the richness of Crazy Quilt fabrics, stitches, and decoration with a striking swastika of black velvet circles and black sateen panels boldly radiating from a black diamond-and-circle cluster at the center (Plate 6). The circles suggest a wheel-of-fortune motif to further extend the symbolic suggestions of luck and chance. The unknown maker at an unknown date used cotton, silk, voided velvet, and etched velvet with uncut pile. The decorative stitches include wheat ear, couching, stem, buttonhole, French knots, herringbone mixed with French knots, and swastika. The swastika stitching combined with French knots figures especially prominently in keeping with the larger overall design superimposed on the basic Crazy Quilt.

Some of the disciplined piecework patterns, such as Roman Stripes and Log Cabin, usually associated with more durable and less extravagant materials, also appear in silks and satins. In addition to the Backus and Tichenor Log Cabin quilts described earlier, the Kentucky Museum has a much worn quilt in the pattern elsewhere identified as Roman Stripes or Roman Squares, each of the alternating five-inch vertical and horizontal blocks containing seven narrow strips. It was made by Mrs. S. M. Matlock of Bowling Green, probably during the nineteenth century. A completed work in the same collection is the familiar Log Cabin squares developed in extra-narrow strips of black silk and magenta velvet. The blocks are arranged in the Barn Raising overall design, and the quilt is backed with mauve brocaded sateen. This is yet another example of a familiar pattern commonly associated with cotton fabrics created here as a parlor throw.

A beautiful velvet quilt in the Doors and Windows pattern (Plate 6) is a treasured possession of Thomas P. Wand of Woodbury, a lifelong resident of Butler County. He recalls watching his mother, Mrs. Elwood (Ginevra Phelps) Wand, piecing the tiny arcs of velvet of many hues around the concave centers of the small blocks until she had accumulated enough for the quilt. "It meant a great deal to her because it was a Friendship Quilt," he explained. "Her friends gave her all the velvet and she made the quilt entirely by hand." Her skillful arrangement of light and dark gives the pattern some of the characteristics of Rob Peter and Pay Paul. Circles created when the blocks were joined were accentuated with briar stitching. The overall pattern lends itself to optical illusions, and the rich reds, blues, greens, browns, and other colors blend harmoniously, somewhat subdued by the use of black in the center areas of many blocks. It is lightly tacked to a lining of red sateen. Mr. Wand does not recall exactly how long his mother worked on the quilt "off and on as people gave her pieces," but he thinks it was completed about 1915.

One dated and signed quilt in the Kentucky Museum displays an unusual example of white hexagons alternating with six-pointed stars (Fig. 37). Although the worn condition of this quilt makes the overall design difficult to illustrate in a photograph, the effect is that of chains of linked circles (really hexagons) of stars. The quilting in the white center areas rivals much regional whitework. A different floral design is quilted into each square and the whole piece is framed with a border of quilted grapevine clusters. In addition to the unusual combination of stars and floral motifs, this quilt displays the sculptured effect created by stuffing. This technique can be achieved in a variety of ways. The most common is to separate carefully the strands of the weave of the backing and push cotton

Figure 37. Detail of Star quilt. Probably the work of Mrs. Edmund Duncan (Temperance Prudence Hutcheson). Note the date quilted at the center of the wreath. Kentucky Museum.

through with a small pointed instrument. One local testimonial refers to a small crochet hook for this operation. After stuffing a section the quilter carefully pushes the threads back together so that there is no trace of the opening.

The Star quilt bears in the quilting the date 1855 and the monogram T.P.H., probably the initials of Temperance Prudence Hutcheson, born in Logan County in 1836 and married to Edmund Duncan in 1855. The obvious inference is that Temperance Prudence lavished great care on what was to become her Bride's Quilt.

An old unfinished scrap found in a box of miscellaneous quilt blocks, also in the Kentucky Museum, provides a good illustration of the patience and time-consuming detail that go into a fancy top. This fragment, date and maker unknown, is a strip of twelve stars set together with small diamonds. The pieces of fine silk in soft pastel shades have been drawn snugly over precisely-cut paper patterns, turned under, and basted. The paper patterns, more substantial than the silk drawn over them, hold the pieces flat for the almost microscopic needlework with which they were assembled. This appears to be a single strand of silk thread whipped into stitches so tight and close that a reading glass is a desirable aid in counting them. This whipstitching is visible on the underside, totally invisible from the top.

The unknown artist apparently intended to embroider a small decorative floral motif into the hexagonal piece at the center of some (or possibly all) of the stars. Two of these have been completed. The design for one of them is sketched in pencil on the back of the paper pattern underlying it. The principal source of the paper patterns appears to have been a ledger or account book. A few pieces contain red parallel lines of the type found in such a book. Bits of information are scattered over the patterns of the assembled strip. The handwritten dates 1853 and 1854 appear, and Glasgow (Kentucky?) appears once. One piece is a fragment of a printed page too small to yield clear information about its source.

The procedure used is clear. The quilter, having decided on a star pattern, made templates for the cloth, allowing for the amount that would be turned under. She then cut out the paper patterns to which she would baste the pieces, a piece of paper for each piece of cloth. Having attached the silk material to the paper with a basting thread, she would sew the six points to the centerpiece of each star. The pattern sketch on the back of one hexagon suggests that the embroidered decorations were applied after the pieces had been assembled.

A scrap of this kind always intrigues the observer. Who was the quilter? And why, after so much work had gone into it, was the strip abandoned? If finished, it would have been a prime example of a conventional piecework pattern done up in an extravagant manner.

Most of the fancy quilts already discussed are to some degree piecework, often with the addition of embroidery and sometimes of applique. Appliqued quilts have their

Figure 38. Center detail of Rose Tree or Tree of Life. Pattern cut out of printed chintz and appliqued to a quilted white background. Susan A. Short, Muhlenberg County, about 1845. Kentucky Museum.

own variations. One technique is to cut out the printed design, ordinarily from printed chintz, and sew it to an elaborately quilted all-white field. The technique is sometimes called Broderie Perse (Persian embroidery) from which many of its motifs are borrowed. One example of this painstaking method is a Rose Tree applique (Fig. 38) made by Mrs. Susan A. Short in Muhlenberg County, probably between 1845 and 1850. The fact that she married in 1848 hints that this may have been a Bride's Quilt. The central portion shows pink roses and four birds of paradise with long tail feathers. The border has floral sprays and each corner has a flowering tree and two birds. The plain backing shows an aristocratic variation of Mrs. Ben Harrison's use of Acme feed sacks—a mirror image of the label "Superfine Shirting." All the elaborate design has been cut out of printed chintz and sewn onto an intricately quilted white background, a technique that was out of style by 1848 but very popular in the 1700s.

A more familiar kind of applique is a nineteenth-century variation of the Whig Rose (Plate 5). Its pink, red, yellow, and green floral design and vining floral border are attached to a closely quilted and stuffed white groundwork. The appliqued floral design is complemented by floral motifs in the quilting. The applique rose, more likely to be called Rose of Sharon, Ohio Rose, or Kentucky Rose by contemporary quilters, is a long-time favorite, as indicated by its earlier Whig label. An especially beautiful quilt in this pattern is among the family heirlooms owned by Frances and Mary Ellen Richards of Franklin. They call it Rose of Sharon. Whatever it is called, it remains a preferred design for keepsake and exhibition.

Appliqued quilts discussed earlier that might be called extravagant include the Mercer County Rose of Sharon and Mrs. Chelf's Oriental Poppy (both Plate 5) and the Simpson County Tulip (Fig. 23). A broader survey would unquestionably bring to light many additional Kentucky-made quilts that would fit into this category.

Fancy quilting and stuffing without contrasting applique or embroidery is called whitework. Its total effect is achieved by elaboration of the process usually considered secondary in pieced quilts, wherein the artistry is expressed in combinations of colored pieces rather than the relatively mechanical process of attaching top and interlining to backing.

Kentucky's most publicized piece of whitework has its title worked into the quilt by its maker: "A Representation of the Fair Ground Near Russellville, Kentucky, 1856" (Figs. 39–41). It is the property of the Smithsonian Institution and certainly it is a worthy representation of the handiwork of a Kentucky artisan for that great national museum. Made in 1856 by Mrs. Virginia Mason Ivey of Logan County, it has been highly praised by various collectors and writers. It is distinctive for the extremely fine detail of realistic representation done entirely in white. The quilt depicts the Fair's exhibition tents sur-

91

Figure 39. "A Representation of the Fair Ground Near Russellville, Kentucky, 1856." Whitework quilt (94″ by 94½″, including fringe) made by Virginia Mason Ivey, Logan County. Photograph courtesy of the Smithsonian Institution, no. 43581-C.

rounded by human figures, livestock, and carriages, with close attention to small details such as harness. The border portrays a never-ending parade of Fair-goers with their horses and carriages, moving along under graceful, exquisitely detailed trees. The background quilting is in a fine stippled effect. Other distinctive features are the effects achieved by stuffing to enhance the relief, and the near-microscopic stitching. Patsy and Myron Orlofsky in *Quilts in America* calculate that this quilt contains 1,200,600 stitches!

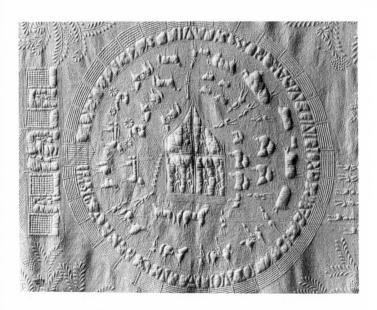

Figure 40 *(above)* Center detail of Russellville Fair Ground quilt, with the title quilted inside the circular fence. Figure 41 *(below)* Border detail. Photographs courtesy of the Smithsonian Institution, nos. 43581-D, E.

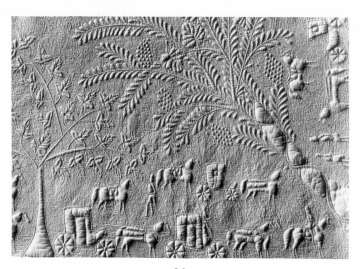

93

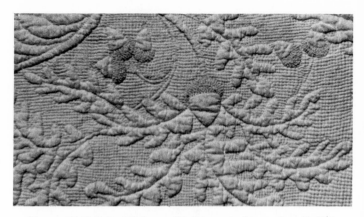

Figure 42. Detail of Rebecca Washington whitework quilt (90″ by 90¾″ overall), completed in 1812. Oak leaves and acorns with French knot caps. Kentucky Museum.

Mrs. Ivey's depiction of the Russellville Fair Ground is an impressive and highly original piece of whitework, but others which rival it as examples of fine needlework remain in Kentucky. An older quilt (Figs. 42–44), also made in Logan County, is one of the prized possessions of the Kentucky Museum. It was finished in 1812 by Mrs. Rebecca Washington, wife of Whiting Washington, whose father was first cousin to George Washington. The Whiting Washington family moved from Virginia to an estate called Green Ridge in Logan County. Museum records indicate that the thread for the quilting and lining was spun and woven at Green Ridge, and the quilt was several years in the frame.

The Washington quilt is in fine condition, lacking only the heavy twelve-inch fringe it had at the time of its completion. Though the decorative motifs are not unusual, the overall design is probably original. A large wreath of grape clusters, leaves, and vines encircles the central area, which is quilted in very small diamonds. An area quilted in small shells separates this from a larger encirclement of acorns, oak leaves, and undulating princess feathers. Separating this from the wide border de-

94

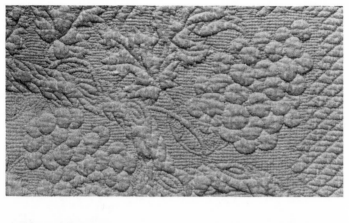

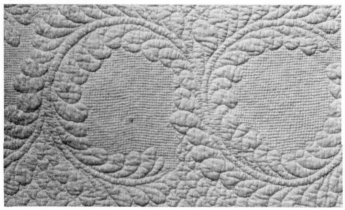

Figure 43 *(top)* Detail of Rebecca Washington whitework quilt, showing popular grape cluster motif and fine corded (trapunto) work. Figure 44 *(above)* Section of border.

sign is another area quilted finely in diamonds with certain areas in shells. The border itself is formed of princess feathers arranged in a row of overlapping wreaths. The Fair Ground quilt is exuberant. The Washington quilt has restraint and a quiet elegance. The tightly crowded French knot acorn caps and the firm stuffing are among the eye-catching features of this his-

95

Figure 45. Center detail of Mercer County whitew, quilt
(104½" by 86" overall). Note the fine trapunto work. Kentucky
Museum.

toric quilt. It was housed at Mt. Vernon early in the
twentieth century but was withdrawn and donated to the
Kentucky Museum in Bowling Green in 1943. Mr. Wythe
Walker of Chicago, who made the presentation, belonged
to the family of Susan Howard Walker of Fayetteville,
Arkansas, the great-granddaughter of the maker of the
quilt. This beautiful and historic quilt frequently appears
in Museum exhibits.

Each all-white quilt has its special points of interest. A
beautiful quilt from Mercer County (Figs. 45, 46), which
reputedly won blue ribbons at all the fairs where it was
exhibited, is said to have required 144 spools of thread for
the groundwork alone. Like many other nineteenth-century quilts, this one has hearts elaborately quilted in the
corners. Grape clusters and leaves encircle a central
star-shaped flower. Corded (trapunto) work in an undulating stemlike (vine?) pattern separates this circle
from a larger one of grape clusters and leaves. Sunflower-
like floral motifs with stems appear at the four corners
between the second circle and the border. Hearts appear

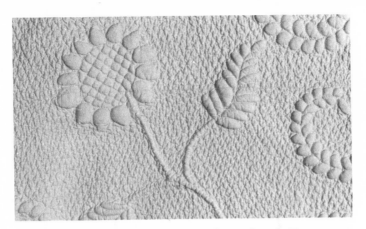

Figure 46. Detail of Mercer County whitework quilt. Trapunto and stuffing set off the flowers and leaf clusters.

at intervals along the border of flowers and elaborately curling wreathlike scrolls which embellish the outer areas of the quilt on all sides.

A peculiarity of this well-executed piece of whitework is that one flower (in a series of similar flowers) has one petal missing. It seems unlikely that this could have been an oversight. A more likely explanation is that the quilter acted upon the belief that an artist should not commit the hubris of striving for total perfection. In that case, a deliberate flaw would be the quilter's confession of mortal frailty.

Another whitework quilt, donated by Embry Smith along with the Temperance Prudence Hutcheson quilt, provides the Kentucky Museum with a handsomely fringed whitework coverlet. The quilting is somewhat less extravagant than on the two quilts described above, which have lost their fringes.

The examples cited thus far lead to an impression that the elaborate or extravagant quilt is no longer favored. To a degree this is true. Some of the fancy quilts already described are commonly called Victorian parlor throws, a clear indication that they are considered out of style. But the elaborately contrived personalized legacy of the quilter is by no means a past institution. Two quilts displayed at a workshop in 1975 show that the tradition continues.

One of these is October Leaves, a beautiful rendition of the multicolored leaves of a Kentucky autumn realistically painted onto a background which harmonizes with the colors. In one corner is embroidered the year of its creation, 1973. Miss Evelyn Fuqua, one of the best-known quilters in Warren County, said the leaves were unusually colorful that year, so she went out and selected typical Kentucky foliage—the bright orange of sassafras, the star-shaped wine red of sweet gum, the flaming orange and crimson of maple, and the nut brown shades of oak. She carried all these and more to her sewing room and attempted to match their colors in textile paints. Then she quilted the designs, outlining each leaf and berry and here and there accentuating leaf veins and stems in the quilting.

October Leaves won second place at the 1975 Hart County Fair. When Miss Fuqua was asked why her quilt had not won a blue ribbon, she replied without false modesty, "Because it didn't meet the exhibit requirement of fitting into one of the specific categories." Then she added with a smile, "Do you know, someone offered me five hundred dollars for that quilt, and I wouldn't take it!" Unfortunately photography does not do justice to the delicate colors of this lovely quilt.

Another example of an extravagantly detailed and highly localized contemporary quilt is a realistic representation of the Bethel Methodist Church outside of Glasgow, Kentucky, on the Burkesville highway (Fig. 47). A church member, Mrs. R. C. Goode, machine-quilted an all-white background diagonally in both directions to yield many uniform diamond-shaped spaces. Into each of these spaces except those in the large central area she embroidered in neat small script the name of a member of the church. Then, with good perspective and

Figure 47. Old Bethel Church quilt. A Name Quilt embroidered by Mrs. R. C. Goode, Glasgow, 1975.

detail, she embroidered a representation of the neat brick church with its tall steeple. Mortar courses between the bricks are represented by fine straight lines of white thread against a field of solid red for the bricks. This quilt was undertaken as a money-making venture for the church. Each member paid a dollar to have his or her name embroidered on the quilt. Mrs. Goode is proud of her ability to achieve a realistic pictorial presentation of the church building. "I think you would recognize the church after you have seen this quilt."

Yet another unusual quilt is equally Kentuckian. A "Jesse Stuart Bookjacket Quilt" was conceived and executed by the W-Hollow author's youngest sister Glennis Stuart Liles, who has been keeping it up to date with the aid of Jesse Stuart's niece Betty Lomiller. The quilt is dated 1958 and bears the names Betty and Glennis. A solid white background was machine-quilted and bound as a possibly reversible quilt. Then the two women began reproducing all Stuart's bookjackets by piecing, appliqued work, and embroidery. Early in 1976 the quilt showed forty-three jackets and seven more were in process. Each one is a little masterpiece of pictorial needlework, from *Man With a Bull-Tongue Plow* to *Come Gentle Spring*. This quilt is usually kept folded at the bottom of an old-fashioned bed in the Stuarts' home, but has been exhibited at the Greenup County Fair and in connection with McGraw-Hill book exhibits.

This chapter has sampled the kinds of quilts that consume both materials and labor far beyond any immediately perceived utilitarian need. In fact, the ostensible function of a quilt, to provide warmth, is partly defeated in some of these extra-fancy creations. Other kinds of need exist, however, and some of them may be even more demanding than the need for physical comfort. The search for a "contented heart" is one of these. The competitive urge to excel in a handicraft, or the need to create a personalized legacy in the best available medium would be still others. Most people feel an urge to brighten their surroundings and act upon it according to current fashion.

For a woman in a nineteenth-century household, virtually confined in the absence of convenient transportation and undisturbed by close neighbors and mass communications, a piece of whitework years in the making could provide an agreeable sense of continuity and stability. Skilled in general needlework through necessity, she could turn at odd hours from prosaic everyday stitchery to the luxury of artwork.

No contemporary quilter contacted in this survey could boast of using 144 spools of thread on one quilt, but many do boast of how many spools or pieces they use. The difference between their extravagant attention to detail and that of quilters a century ago seems to be a matter of degree.

5

BY ANY OTHER NAME

THE DELIGHTFUL whimsicality expressed in quilt-naming, that carefree riot of verbal creations matching to some degree the visual creations they name, disturbs quilters and quilt-lovers not at all. The seekers after "correct" names in neat categories may find their efforts more frustrating than fruitful. Names of quilt patterns, like names of old songs and favorite recipes that are passed around informally, proliferate and overlap—continually re-emerging, recombining, here and there appearing in print as they show minor variations under new and old names.

A student struggling with what seemed to her irresponsibly inconsistent behavior on the part of English grammar remarked, "I wish English was more like Latin—you can count on Latin!" From her point of view it seemed that there should be one right and unconfusing way to say a thing. Quilt-naming is a good deal more like English in this respect, for very few quilt names can be "counted on" to apply to one and only one pattern, any more than a quilt pattern can be counted on to have only one name. As the Orlofskys point out in *Quilts in America* (p. 245), "Legends thrive concerning origins of quilt patterns and names; however, little or no documentary evidence emerges in letters, diaries, inventories, and other historical records." The failure of the Orlofskys' quest for certainties on this subject neither proves nor disproves any particular point. Researchers on place names, oral historians, and folklorists will continue the quest even as they yield to a certain charm in its elusiveness.

Though never the primary consideration of the maker or user of quilts, quilt-naming has its own mystique. Now and again, just as the craftsmanship and design reveal the hand or eye of the artist, quilt names reveal a touch of the poet.

"Well, I call it Dove in the Window," Flora Free said of the pattern she enjoyed giving as a wedding gift. One of the initiated, she was fully aware that her pattern probably was traveling under a number of aliases. Carrie Hall in *The Romance of the Patchwork Quilt in America* calls this pattern Weathervane on the authority of a quilter of an earlier time and another place. Flora Free's name is the right one for her quilt (Fig. 22). The best authority is the maker, surely, and throughout this discussion the first designation for any quilt described or pictured has been the name its maker gave it, if known.

Some names of geometric or pictorial patterns are reasonably descriptive, at least the generic part of the name, such as Hexagon, House, or Star. By far the majority of them tend to be imaginative, evocative, or downright puzzling, yet a name may lead others to see with the namer a resemblance not seen before. Inspiration comes from nature, daily life, history, the Bible, and that limitless realm of moods, attitudes, and values that makes the names as well as the quilts themselves "time capsules," as a writer for *Antiques* (vol. 100, p. 162) once described them.

Names once clearly symbolic may, like the pattern and quilting motifs, alter or lose their meaning with the passage of time. As the twentieth century wanes, so may old implications of names and patterns. But unless romance is lost, vestiges of symbolic meaning will continue, like legend, to be part of Kentucky's quilting story. Not by

Figure 48. One block of I Wish You Well, Ellen Barrow's name for the swastika pattern in her family tradition. The same two shapes are used for this pattern as for Drunkard's Path shown in Figure 18.

chance did swastikas appear on so many nineteenth-century quilts, even in the fancy stitching of the silk and velvet couch throws of the Victorian era. It is certain that the quilt-makers knew the symbolism of that age-old good luck motif. Ellen Barrow may not use the word swastika at all, but when her son inquired the name of a quilt on his bed with interesting looking plump-armed swastikas (Fig. 48), she answered, "I Wish You Well." Puzzled, he repeated his question, but her first answer was correct. Another of her favorite patterns suggesting a luck motif is Wheel of Fortune. Both I Wish You Well and Wheel of Fortune are from the Muntz family repertory.

Double Wedding Ring, Lover's Knot, Friendship Knot, and Friendship Circle speak clearly even to the uninitiated. Tree of Life and Tree of Paradise vie with Pine Tree, all three names applied to similar patterns within a small region; the first two are red in some repertories instead of the usual Pine Tree green. With the exception of Wedding Ring, these patterns have other names, and the names apply to other patterns.

A once-common quilt name that seems to have disappeared from the Kentucky region is Wandering Foot, but most quilters across the state recognize the pattern as Turkey Tracks. An old belief—that if a young man slept under a Wandering Foot quilt he would become a wanderer—may have influenced the change.

Some quilt names still keep their religious overtones. The Rose of Sharon variations throughout the history of Kentucky quilting suggest the delicately colored but hardy flower of that name that has grown beside so many kitchen doors; but the name evoked from one modern quilter the comment, "That's in the Bible, you know." Job's Patience from Hart County and Joseph's Coat from many counties explain themselves and fit the medium of quilt-making. Devil's Backbone hints more at humor than at religious connotations. Crown of Thorns (which applies to more than one pattern used by Kentucky quilters), Star of the East, Star of Bethlehem, Heavenly Star, and Cathedral Windows suggest religious awe. The name that Miriam Tuska applies to a stark array of dark right-angled triangles leaning against a white background has an austere appropriateness—Tents of Armageddon.

Throughout Kentucky the Bible exerts direct as well as traditional influence on quilt-naming. "Scripture Quilts" in a range of stenciled, painted, and embroidered types appear. An Edmonson County quilter who had one in her quilting hoops in 1971 when the author paid her a visit called it her New Testament Quilt. Reminiscent of religious calendar art and old Sunday School cards, these quilts are seldom original creations, nor are their names.

A whole family of quilt patterns share the name Rob Peter and Pay Paul (also called Robbing Peter to Pay Paul), a blend of Biblical and Quaker influences. The

Figure 49. Section of Lover's Knot. Annie Chelf, Jonesville, contemporary.

name derives not from shapes but from a shared principle of alternating two sharply contrasting colors in an overlapping design so that the major color of one block becomes the minor color of the next. An example is a block shaped like the broad outline of Improved Nine-Patch. Mrs. Chelf called her red and white quilt in this pattern Rob Peter and Pay Paul (Fig. 11). In one block the central motif is red, the outline white; in the next block the red "robs" the white for outline and the white "robs" the red for the center. The principle of alternating and overlapping then suggests the name, and its applications can be a source of confusion for the novice. If Mrs. Chelf had made her quilt in orange she might have called it Orange Peel. Carrie Hall pictured on the same page three patterns for the name Rob Peter and Pay Paul. Of these, one has been called Steeplechase, another Melon Patch (which is used for other patterns, including a beautiful applique design credited to Kentucky), and yet another is called Drunkard's Path (Fig. 18), this name more common for it in Kentucky than Rob Peter and Pay Paul. Any pattern

Figure 50. Section of Jacob's Ladder. Pieced by Mae Young and quilted by Ellen Barrow. Author's collection.

that permits the lend and borrow arrangement of alternating positive and negative images (such as Lover's Knot, Fig. 49) may somewhere be called Rob Peter and Pay Paul.

A traditional pattern that Kentucky quilters call Jacob's Ladder (Fig. 50), with slight variations in the color harmony, has inspired a whole group of Rocky Road designations. Whether the Rocky Road be to Dublin, California, Georgia, Kansas, Oklahoma, or the White House—all these have been attached to the pattern somewhere by Kentucky quilters. They agree upon the use of two colors for Jacob's Ladder, three or more for their Rocky Roads. Carrie Hall notes that the pattern was once known as Underground Railroad in western Kentucky, a name that seems to have disappeared since the publication of her book in the 1930s. The Rocky Road names attach to some other patterns, but with much less frequency. Ellen Barrow referred to the pattern generally known in the region as Drunkard's Path or Drunkard's Trail as the Rocky Road to Durbin's. This appears to be a localizing for Dublin, since Durbin is a well-known family name in her area, where even in the 1970s rocky roads may lead to homes of rural friends. The name Durbin's also designates a Bowling Green store that for many years catered to quilters' needs.

The quilter is usually more patriotic than political in her name allusions to historical personages, places, and events. When asked why her Thomas Jefferson quilt was called that, Mae Young replied simply, "That's just its name." The Muhlenberg County quilt enthusiast who bought Battle of Tippecanoe at a Kentucky auction for five dollars was aware of the hard-fought election that gave rise to the Tippecanoe slogan, but was more delighted to have an unusual quilt at a bargain price. Washington's Plumes, a swastika-like wheel pattern that survives in some repertories, and Mrs. Chelf's Lincoln quilt may keep their names for a time.

A once-popular name was Star of LeMoyne, an eighteenth-century quilt namer's tribute to the brothers who founded the city of New Orleans. To all except the most book-oriented quilters the pattern has become Lemon Star or some other star name that requires no knowledge of history for its interpretation.

A young woman brought to a quilting workshop a quilt block for a pattern she wanted to make, certain that one of the more experienced quilters could tell her its name. "Star of the West," one said, and another called it Pinwheel. But the majority ruled, and she will call it Clay's Choice, although the name will not mean to her what it meant to her great-grandmother, who lived in the time of Kentucky's great Whig leader, Henry Clay. Even in that era prior to women's active role in politics, grandmother would have been aware of Clay's fiery Senate debates with South Carolina's John C. Calhoun and of the magnetism and power that twice brought him close to his party's nomination for the presidency.

Whig's Defeat and Whig Rose were meaningful in that same era, and Kentucky quilters probably participated in the nineteenth-century controversy over which political party—Whig or Democrat—had the right to be identified with one of the most beautiful of all applique rose patterns (Plate 5). On twentieth-century quilts Whig Rose may merge with or revert to the older Rose of Sharon designation; it may attach to some geographical area (Ohio Rose); or it may come to be called simply Rose Applique. The broken circle pattern embellished with tiny sawtooth diamonds which appeared throughout Kentucky as Whig's Defeat (Fig. 15) may lose its old name altogether and take on the happier title of Indian Summer or something even more informal, such as Fanny's Favorite.

The Log Cabin quilts, with names like Barn Raising and Courthouse Steps, evoke nostalgic images rather than specific events, as do all those Rocky Roads and household objects like Churn Dash, Flat Iron, and Monkey Wrench (a favorite of Dixie Lee of Butler County). Identification of quilt names with particular historical events or persons may persist elsewhere in Kentucky, but in the region studied this does not seem to be a trend.

Just as the "Lemon" Star breaks its tie with history, so Dresden Plate undergoes an interesting emancipation from geography as it travels under the names Dressen, Dessert, and Drazling, or moves all the way to Friendship Ring. All those Fan and Basket names, all the Fruit and Flower names evoke a woman's world of house and garden, of joy in everyday things and beauty in nature. The most fervent champion of women's rights could hardly object to what the names reflect—that the activity persists because it gives happiness. Again, why?

Miriam Tuska, with her appreciation of the artistic effects some quilters achieve, says "A quilt that reaches me must be strong in design quality. It must have vitality." She points to her Tents of Armageddon, to her angular Basket Quilts, and to the ingenious work of Log Cabin quilt-makers. "The names don't matter," she says. But even her own labels as she exhibits her quilts and lectures about them sound like poetry: Mosaic in Diamonds, Mountain Homespun, Flying Geese, and Snow Crystals. And she describes one from Cynthiana, pictured in her *Antiques* article, as "frenzied, almost cubist—like a fractured painting." She calls it "Jewel Crazy Quilt."

The quilt-makers and namers may not verbalize Mrs. Tuska's appreciation, and they visualize the quilt as a whole on a bed rather than hanging on the wall like a painting. But the names they choose show that they too respond to the optical illusions of movement and the changing patterns created when their quilts are viewed in their full glory—names like Ocean Waves, Windmill, Blazing Star, and Sunburst; names like Mule quilt, Redbird in the Corner, Snake Trail, and (Trip) Around the World.

The language of a highly organized activity with a hierarchy of authority does not grow with such abandon. A scientific society or a union of craft workers by its very existence exerts pressure on its members to speak the "official" language. But quilting is different. Its language has for centuries been an indicator of the popularity and informality of the craft.

Not only patterns but also quilting equipment appears under a variety of names. For example, frame as used in this book refers to the total equipment for framing the cloth sandwich during the quilting phase. But many Kentucky quilters say frames or set of frames, and some vary from frame to frames according to context. The hanging frame for some is a swinging frame. A standing frame may be referred to as trestle, horse, or sawhorse frame (or frames). For the pieces to which the lining is attached, the author has rather arbitrarily chosen rails, which is a term no more commonly used than bars, sides, poles, or boards.

The quilter's activities and the quilting designs have variable names, too. "Laying out the quilt" (or sometimes "laying off the quilt") means the same thing as marking the design for quilting. Diagonal lines of quilting are bias lines, slant lines, or simply diagonals. If they cross in opposite directions, the quilter may say she crossed the bias lines or that she quilted in diamonds. A combination of vertical and horizontal lines may be described as checks or squares. When a quilter crosses a piece or a block, she may form an X or a cross. Square fans are formed of a series of half-squares or right angles, akin to round fans formed of quarter circle arcs (in some quilting manuals called shells). To regional quilters shells are quite different from fans. Even the popular practice of quilting by pattern may be synonymous with quilting by the piece or by the block.

The filler or batting, because it was so long made of cotton, is still "a cotton" to some quilters, even if it is made of dacron. It may also be a fill, a stuffing, or a batt. (The term wadding that appears elsewhere has not found favor in south-central Kentucky.)

Some of the variant terms involved with preparing the quilt top have been discussed earlier, with special attention to piece and patch. "Stripping the blocks together" usually means separating the blocks with narrow strips of contrasting material, but it can be synonymous with setting the quilt together. One quilter used the phrase "chased the squares together" to express her sewing of interlocking triangles to join the blocks into quilt-length strips, then referred to combining the strips as "setting it together."

Family groups, neighborhood homemakers' groups, church organizations, or even individual quilters may develop their own naming to some degree for their tools, processes, and patterns. Naming, then, is one more facet of the quilter's ingenuity and creativity.

In 1975 Arizona Martin in her ninth decade sat at a kitchen table cutting out quilt pieces with her daughter. The two quilters exchanged information about patterns, nieces, grandchildren, and neighbors. Arizona learned only that day the name of a pattern she had admired,

Goose in the Pond. She decided to "take off" the pattern and try it. This was a typical face-to-face exchange. Quilting is a performance in which one person shows another in small groups—families, neighbors, churches, community clubs.

Even at a workshop set up by an extension home economist, quilters bring their quilts, quilt blocks, and unfinished tops, which they show each other in clusters of two's and three's after the brief formalities of introduction. The home economist wisely sets up this show-and-tell opportunity, recognizing her role as catalyst more than instructor and bowing to the authority of the experienced quilter showing an eager learner how to fold and tack the layers of cloth to make the intricate Cathedral Windows.

Commercial patterns and quilting manuals follow, rather than lead, this traditional informal performance. Thousands of Kentuckians in 1976 practice this ancient craft with undiminished enthusiasm, not in an ephemeral fad of popular culture, but in a grassroots continuity that responds to fads by absorbing and refining them.

Selected Sources

Bacon, Lenice Ingram. *American Patchwork Quilts*. Birmingham, Alabama: Oxmoor House, 1973.

Finley, Ruth. *Old Patchwork Quilts and the Women Who Made Them*. Newton Centre, Massachusetts: Charles T. Branford, 1971.

Hall, Carrie A., and Kretsinger, Rose. *The Romance of the Patchwork Quilt in America*. New York: Bonanza Books, n.d. Reprint of 1935 edition of Caxton Printers, Ltd., Caldwell, Idaho.

Hall, Eliza Calvert. *Aunt Jane of Kentucky*. A. L. Burt Company, 1907.

———. *A Book of Handwoven Coverlets*. New York: Little, Brown and Company, 1912.

Hinson, Dolores A. *A Quilting Manual*. New York: Hearthside Press, 1970.

Holstein, Jonathan. *The Pieced Quilt*. Greenwich, Connecticut: New York Graphic Society, Ltd., 1973.

Ickis, Marguerite. *The Standard Book of Quilt Making and Collecting*. New York: Dover Publications, 1959.

Kentucky Building Library and Museum, Western Kentucky University, Bowling Green.

McKim, Ruby. *One Hundred and One Patchwork Patterns*. New York: Dover Publications, 1962.

Orlofsky, Patsy, and Orlofsky, Myron. *Quilts in America*. New York: McGraw-Hill Book Company, 1974.

Pforr, Effie Chalmers. *Award Winning Quilts*. Birmingham, Alabama: Oxmoor House, 1974.

Safford, Carleton L., and Bishop, Robert. *America's Quilts and Coverlets*. New York: E. P. Dutton and Company, 1972.

Tuska, Miriam Gittleman. "Kentucky Quilts." *Antiques*, April 1974, pp. 784–90.

Webster, Marie D. *Quilts: Their Story and How to Make Them.* New York: Tudor Publishing Company, 1948.

Western Kentucky University Folklore and Folklife Collection, Cravens Graduate Center, Bowling Green.

Index to Quilt-Makers

Index to Pattern Names